TCCB

The Test and County Cricket Board Collection

CRICKET

◄ HEROES ►

TCCB

The Test and County Cricket Board Collection

CRICKET

◄ HEROES ►

ESSAYS ON ENGLAND'S FINEST PLAYERS
BY ENGLAND'S FINEST WRITERS

Edited by Peter Hayter

BLOOMSBURY

Sports Editions Limited

Managing Director	Richard Dewing
Art Director	Mary Hamlyn
Senior Designer	Rob Kelland
Designers	Sandra Cowell
	Adrian Waddington
Editor	Leslie Smillie
Picture Research	Sandra Cowell
	Abigail Sims

First published in 1990 by
Bloomsbury Publishing Limited
2 Soho Square
London
W1V 5DE

ISBN 0-7475-0508-X

Produced, edited and designed by
Sports Editions Limited
3 Greenlea Park
Prince George's Road
London
SW19 2JD

Typeset in Bodoni and 20th Century by Sports Editions Limited

Origination, printing and binding by Butler and Tanner, Frome

Cover illustrations of Boycott, Dexter, Gower, Compton, Trueman, Botham and Grace by Gavin Harrison

c r i c k e t   h e r o e s

PREFACE

There are two ways, it seems to me, to go about the business of books. First, there is the hard way, writing them yourself. Then there is the easy way, having other people write them for you. In this respect, my involvement in this book represents a triumph for the easy way.

Cricket Heroes belongs not to me, but to the writers and, more importantly, to the cricketers who made it worth writing. Cricket, more than any other sport, thrives on the written word. Through the years, men such as C. L. R. James, Neville Cardus, Jack Fingleton and R. C. Robertson-Glasgow built reputations not as cricket writers but as writers who wrote about cricket. They set the standard by which all others are judged. What typified their work was the implicit understanding that the game is an avenue of expression for the human character. I hope that what you read of the work of those who have followed indicates that the same rules still apply.

I would like to thank the writers; Tim Crow of the Test and County Cricket Board for his enthusiasm and invaluable assistance; Geoffrey Copinger for providing the statistics for each player; Leslie Smillie and Matthew Hamlyn; Sandra Cowell for her diligent picture research; all the photographers whose work illuminates the book; and Mary Hamlyn and her team of designers.

Finally, I would like to thank my father, Reg Hayter, for helping me to appreciate cricket and cricket writing.

Peter Hayter
St Kitts
February 1990

CONTENTS

CONTENTS

cricket heroes

LES AMES

Tony Pawson

Leslie Ethelbert George Ames was a Kentish legend in the great Kentish tradition of wicket-keeper batsmen of Test class. With Huish and Hubble as fine exemplars for him to follow, Ames developed his own inimitable style just as Godfrey Evans and Alan Knott were later to develop theirs. As a wicket-keeper Ames adopted the Quaker philosophy of studying to be quiet and impeccably correct. No raucous Duckworth-type appeals from him, nor any of Evans's flamboyance, nor of Knott's acrobatic agility. One bail removed and a polite enquiry of the umpire was the Ames approach.

One bail removed was a hallmark also of a different era of cricket in which great spinners flourished and the wicket-keeping job was inevitably more demanding and more important. The most remarkable of all such combinations was that of 'Tich' Freeman and Les Ames. When Freeman took an incredible 304 wickets in a season in 1928, the 300th victim was Richard Tyldesley, appropriately stumped by Ames. Of Ames's 842 victims while playing for Kent, 512 were caught and 330 stumped. The modern difference is well expressed by only 87 of Alan Knott's total of 915 being stumped.

The MCC Coaching Book laid it down as an unarguable principle that the best wicket-keeper must always be chosen regardless of batting ability. That was sensible enough in Ames's day, but is outdated in the present game. The emphasis on speed and the virtual elimination of true wrist spin means that English 'keepers stand back most of the time and the vast majority of chances are easy by comparison with standing up to spinners. So it became sensible to include the likes of Jim Parks in a Test team when his batting so improved the balance of the side that it outweighed the fact that he was not in the top six 'keepers in the country. Alan Knott's superior batting also ensured his place as of right, making him first choice for many years despite the matching talent of Bob Taylor as a world-class 'keeper.

Happily no such decision ever had to be made about Ames since the selectors could confidently pick him as the best 'keeper and as also worth his place as a batsman. 2,434 runs in 47 Tests for an impressive average of 40.56 was proof enough of that, as was the tally of 74 caught and 23 stumped of his main skill. There was an added value to his batting in the textbook purity of his stroke

cricket heroes

LES AMES

play, the attraction of his powerful straight driving and the speed of his scoring. Three of the best examples of that are Ames's swift 202 not out in Kent's record total of 803 for 4 made in seven hours against Essex at Brentwood in 1934, coming in after Ashdown and Woolley had put on 352 in the highest ever partnership for Kent — a massacre of tired bowling. Gloucestershire's attack was fresh enough when Ames hit 70 in just 36 minutes as Kent scored 219 for 2 in 71 minutes to race to a win at Dover in August 1937. The different attitude of those days is clear from Tom Goddard's analysis of 8.2 overs for 98 runs. Who today would allow a slow bowler to continue like that when opponents have a race against the clock? In Tests there was his remarkable partnership with 'Gubby' Allen against New Zealand in 1931 as 246 runs in under three hours transformed the score from 190 for 7, with Ames making 137.

Les Ames behind the stumps for Kent against Sussex in 1932. He made a remarkable total of 441 stumpings in his career.

Les had been educated at the Harvey Grammar School in Folkestone and it was at Folkestone that he made 295 against Gloucestershire, his highest score. That was in 1933, his best batting season, when he totalled 3,058 runs. When I started to play for Kent after the war either Evans or Levett kept wicket while Ames was our premier batsman and occasional bowler of crafty legbreaks. Oh yes, Les could bowl as well, with 24 wickets at an average of 33.37. The most amusing of these was seeing him beat and bowl Mike Ainsworth on 99 — Mike certainly didn't think it funny as he had been promised a special present if he made a century.

Cricket statistics can be worse than damned lies if they take no regard of conditions or opposition strength. Yet just as Bradman's extraordinary Test average makes it a waste of time to indulge in any argument about who is the best batsman of all time so Les's run totals, batting first wicket down for Kent, indicate just how good he was then. In both 1947 and 1949 he topped two thousand runs despite being in his forties and plagued by occasional back trouble. That trouble had cost him a season's cricket in 1936 and was to bring

cricket heroes

LES AMES

an abrupt termination to his playing career in 1951. His overall record would be even more remarkable but for the years lost to the war and a bad back.

My happiest memory of batting with him was in a partnership at Canterbury which set up a win over Middlesex with seven minutes to spare and also brought him his hundredth hundred to spark a delighted cacophony from the hooting horns and the cheering crowd. His straight driving was a wonder to behold that day as three men on the boundary behind the bowler hardly touched the ball as it flew over or between them, so powerful was his hitting, so accurate his placing. His 131 in two hours won the match with my own 57 contributing to a partnership of 85 in 37 minutes.

Les was born at Elham on 3rd December 1905 and as a youngster was soon absorbing the unique atmosphere of the Canterbury weeks of those days with the tents, the bands, and the added colour of Ladies Day. My father, himself a first-class wicket-keeper who was four years in the Oxford side, claimed that he spotted Les's potential in a club game and told the County. The truth is that the potential was so obvious anyone could spot it and in 1926 Les played his first two matches for the County, taking four catches in one of them — in the outfield.

Next year he had his first relatively full season, beginning to take over from Hubble as 'keeper and scoring more than a thousand runs. With G. B. Legge succeeding A. J. Evans as captain, Kent finished as runners-up in 1928 largely due to the partnership of Ames and Freeman. That was the year 'Tich' took 304 wickets, 246 of them for Kent, while Ames in all caught 69 and stumped 52, a record. Next year Ames went six better in victims, his brilliance soon being accorded the recognition which was to bring him 47 Test caps.

In 1928 he played for an England XI against a West Indies team defeated already in the Tests. His score of 42 was the highest in the first innings, with Woolley winning the match with an inspired second innings 151. His Kent colleagues Woolley and Freeman were also primarily responsible for winning the third and fourth Tests against South Africa the following year which allowed the selectors to displace Duckworth at last — and give Ames his chance (Ames had been on the winter tour to Australia, but was not picked for any Test). Les was out for a duck, but his keeping was as cool and impeccable as ever.

LES AMES

By the time of the famous (or infamous according to your viewpoint) 'bodyline' series the roles were reversed with Duckworth the permanent reserve. Les did score 69 at Adelaide, but otherwise it was his keeping, rather than his batting, which produced impressive results. Not so in 1934 against Australia. He and Leyland just failed to save the first Test with a courageous 70 minute stand against Bill O'Reilly, who was almost unplayable on a crumbling pitch. Ames's 120 in the next Test contributed to squaring the series, with Australia beaten by an innings as Verity took 15 wickets on a rain-damaged pitch. Ames caught Bradman off a skier with the great man never at his best on a difficult wicket, and out to a wild slog just as the pitch was easing.

The fifth Test was the decider and so a timeless one. That suited Bradman and Ponsford, who launched Australia to victory with individual scores of 244 and 266. In the England reply Ames himself was well set on 33 when he ricked his back and had to retire. This gave Kent another wicket-keeping record, albeit unwelcome. Frank Woolley took over behind the stumps and let a record number of byes to add to the misery of a final Test in which he scored 4 and 0.

Ames's contribution to cricket was far from being confined to his playing days. These ended sadly at the very start of the 1951 season. In the first match against Nottinghamshire at Gillingham Ames was in pain after ricking his back again when fielding. He had not meant to bat, but six wickets fell quickly. Courageous and committed as always Les struggled to the wicket. In his own words he then "went to play a ball round to leg and just collapsed in a heap. It was my last game."

So there was no nostalgic farewell match and the tributes were reserved for later. A special feature article in the County's annual read: "It was not only what Les Ames did, but the way he did it, which will mark him for all time as one of the finest exponents of the game of cricket. His whole-hearted enthusiasm and extraordinary efficiency were only equalled by his personal modesty. He might have earned his place in any team by his wicket-keeping or his batting alone, but he had not the single-mindedness of the specialist. Always a great-hearted player, his best efforts were at the disposal of the captain as long as the game was in progress."

Those achievements were recognised by his being elected an Honorary Life Member of the MCC — a rare distinction for a professional, and a Life-Member

c r i c k e t   h e r o e s

LES AMES

of Kent. That county he continued to serve, being Manager in 1957 and later a very shrewd Secretary/Manager, helping Kent to a period of success. Appropriately he went out this time on a high note, retiring in 1974 after Kent won the Gillette Cup. The Kent connection continued, though, through the Hoppers Tie Club, of which he remained controller until his death in February of this year. This was inaugurated by Les, Bryan Valentine and 'Hopper' Levett when the County produced a tie which the players were not allowed to wear.

One of the shrewdest England captains under whom Les played was Bob Wyatt. His view of Ames was unequivocal: "The best batsman/wicket-keeper England has ever possessed. Makes few mistakes behind the wicket and is particularly quick when stumping. He is a forceful batsman who is very quick on his feet and a good player of slow bowling. Drives well and is a fine exponent of the on-drive. He is also a fine slip and very quick in the outfield."

In cricket terms and as a man Ames was indeed a Jack of all trades, and Master of all.

L. E. G. AMES   KENT
BORN 3.12.05, ELHAM, KENT

BATTING

	Matches	Innings	Not out	Runs	High score	Avg	100
Test	47	72	12	2,434	149	40.56	8
First class	593	951	95	37,248	295	43.51	102

BOWLING AND FIELDING

	Runs	Wickets	Avg	5 W/I	10 W/M	BB	Ct	St
Test	0	0	0	0	0	0	74	23
First class	801	24	33.37	0	0	3/23	703	418

TREVOR BAILEY

John Woodcock

In the 1950s Trevor Bailey became a symbol of resistance. When England were in trouble on the cricket field, people would say: "It'll be all right, Bailey's still there." It was a reputation based more on intense application than great natural ability, and it had its origins at Lord's on June 30th 1953, when, with Willie Watson of Yorkshire, he shared in one of the greatest of all match-saving partnerships.

It has to be remembered that those were the days when a Test Match between England and Australia had the whole country by the ears — much as happens in Australia now for the running of the Melbourne Cup. The market had yet to be flooded with one-day internationals. In 1953 it was 15 years and a World War since England had beaten Australia, and longer than that since they had held the Ashes. Another defeat seemed imminent when, with England 73 for four in their second innings and still 269 runs adrift, Bailey joined Watson 50 minutes before lunch on the last day at Lord's. When the next wicket fell it was nearly six o'clock and England were safe.

Next morning the *Manchester Guardian* led its front page with Neville Cardus's report, headlined 'Miracle of Faith at Lord's.' Someone else came up with 'Barnacle Bailey.' When, later in the same series, Bailey denied Australia for a second time — by batting 4 hours and 20 minutes for 38 and then using every device to hold them up with the ball — he became a marked man. The last ditch was his spiritual home, and no-one was to come to know it better than the Australians.

The forward defensive stroke was Trevor's trademark, the bat well out in front of the pad rather than wedged against it as it would be today. As a bowler, he gave thought to every ball. Close to the wicket he held some brilliant catches. In his first-class career he scored 28,641 runs, took 2,082 wickets, caught 428 batsmen and stonewalled countless thousands of spectators into a state of stupor. In 215 of his 1,072 innings he finished not out, and if, in doing so, he had saved a seemingly lost cause, he went to bed a happy man.

Born at Westcliff-on-Sea on December 3rd, 1923, Bailey was fortunate to be coached at his preparatory school by Denys Wilcox, who had captained Cambridge and Essex, and then at Dulwich College by C. S. Marriott, who had

Trevor Bailey in 1953, the year in which he featured in a match-saving partnership with Willie Watson for England.

TREVOR BAILEY

bowled leg breaks for Kent and once for England. Bailey had five years in the Dulwich side, combining with A. W. H. Mallett in 1941 and 1942 to make them more than a match for the schools they played. While in the Royal Marines from 1943 until 1946 the name he had made for himself at school meant that he was on the mailing list for war-time matches at Lord's when stationed within reach. He was in the Cambridge sides of 1947 and 1948, and played the first of his 61 Test Matches, against New Zealand, in 1949. Once in the England side he stayed there without a break, other than for the occasional injury or when MCC went to India or Pakistan, until the end of the tour to Australia in 1958-59.

His career with Essex ran from 1946 until 1967. At different times he was assistant secretary, secretary and captain. If he was not in his office, which was a caravan for much of the summer, he was usually to be found batting or bowling. He and Doug Insole, who had first played together at Cambridge, were at that time the style and substance of Essex cricket — they gave it its stability and character — but despite their best efforts the county championship eluded them.

Bailey did the double of 1,000 runs and 100 wickets eight times. Since 1937 he stands alone in having scored 2,000 runs and taken 100 wickets in a season (1959). He is one of only four Englishmen to have scored more than 2,000 runs and taken over 100 wickets in Test cricket. He was what all successful Test sides need, unless they have a pack of very fast bowlers, namely a genuine all-rounder. Of the five series he played in against Australia, England won three.

Having opened the bowling in his first Test Match, at Headingley, he opened the batting in his last, at Melbourne. When, at Melbourne, Ray Lindwall yorked him in the second innings, it meant a 'pair' for Bailey but took the great Lindwall past Clarrie Grimmett's previous Australian record of 215 Test wickets. Lindwall paid Bailey the compliment of saying that the record felt all the better for having fallen as it did. For Bailey aroused in his opponents a powerful, if sometimes grudging, respect. I am sure West Indians of his own generation would agree with that. Having bowled them out by the evening of the first day of the last Test Match at Kingston, Jamaica, in 1953-54, he then added insult to injury by going in first with his captain, Len Hutton, and still

Another ovation for Bailey, this time following a crucial 38 scored in 260 minutes to save England from defeat.

TREVOR BAILEY

being there at close of play 35 minutes later. Less helpfully, his 68 in seven hours and 38 minutes against Australia at Brisbane in 1958-59 did a good deal more for Australia's morale than England's.

To younger generations it must seem strange that with his sharp eye for the game he was never seriously canvassed for the England captaincy. If he were playing today, he certainly would be. As it is, he commentates knowingly and nasally, but never noisily, for the BBC, moves genially around the cricket scene, and simply hates to see an England side failing for want of a disciplined approach. He would have been a fiendishly effective one-day bowler, and no bad one-day batsman. At Brisbane in 1954-55, when an Australian philanthropist offered £100 to the first Englishman to hit a six, Bailey very soon won the money. He was, you understand, nothing if not deliberate.

In the nets at Chingford, Essex getting in some batting practice.

T. E. BAILEY ESSEX
BORN 3.12.23, WESTCLIFF-ON-SEA, ESSEX

BATTING

	Matches	Innings	Not out	Runs	High score	Avg	100
Test	61	91	14	2,290	134*	29.74	1
First class	682	1,072	215	28,641	205	33.42	28

BOWLING AND FIELDING

	Runs	Wickets	Avg	5 W/I	10 W/M	BB	Ct	St
Test	3,856	132	29.21	5	1	7/34	32	0
First class	48,170	2,082	23.13	110	13	10/90	428	0

c r i c k e t   h e r o e s

SYDNEY BARNES

Brian Bearshaw

No man has gone into English cricket history with such a high reputation from so little county and Test experience as Sydney Barnes. He played 46 times for Lancashire, four for Warwickshire and 27 for England in a first-class career which extended over 37 seasons and which brought him 719 wickets at 17.09 each in 133 games. But it should be remembered that he played without the daily grind of county cricket which can so easily bring on staleness. Perhaps Barnes, like many Test cricketers, would have had to ration his energies if he had played 400 times for Lancashire instead of 46, as well as playing for England, and maybe his record would not have been the formidable one it is. He found the daily demands of county cricket too irksome, and settled, instead, for the gentler requirements of league and Minor Counties cricket where he could take wickets by the sackful without breaking into a sweat.

Barnes was born in Smethwick in Staffordshire on April 19, 1873, and did not take up cricket seriously until he joined his town team at the age of 18. He received little coaching but soon learned to bowl off breaks and leg breaks at a fast-medium pace. He had a perfect action, a springy run-up with his arm straight and as high as possible at the point of delivery. He had an impeccable length and a line which made batsmen play every ball. And he spun the ball sharply. Don Bradman once argued that Bill O'Reilly had claims to a higher position than Barnes among history's great bowlers. "O'Reilly had all the tricks of Barnes, plus one which Barnes hadn't — the googly," said Bradman. Neville Cardus told Barnes about Bradman's opinion. "He's quite right," said Barnes, "I didn't bowl the googly. I never needed it."

Barnes played a little for Warwickshire before becoming a professional in the Lancashire League where he found the games played in a different spirit to that he had been accustomed to in the Birmingham League. He was not used to that extra keenness to win, a keenness that got into his system because he felt everything depended on him. It was this spirit, he thought, which made him a fighter and a perfectionist. And which made him so unpopular, even among his fellow players. He himself later admitted: "I was a difficult man to play with. I did my best at all times and expected the others to do the same." And when they did not, he fumed and raged.

SYDNEY BARNES

Len Hopwood, who played for Lancashire between the wars, remembered playing for Lancashire 2nd XI against a Staffordshire side which included Barnes — and an amiable parson who was not worth his place but who was being rewarded for his enthusiasm and loyalty to club cricket. To his horror the parson found himself at silly point, a member of the clan which Barnes had gathered around the batsman on the turning wicket. As Barnes ran up to bowl, the parson craftily retreated until Barnes came to a halt halfway through his run-up and put the fear of God into the unfortunate man with a blistering verbal castigation, which was followed by a demonstration of where to stand plus a strict instruction to stay there. The next ball was a rank long hop outside the off stump which the batsman, Len Hopwood, crashed to the boundary, missing the parson, and a possible homicide, by inches. A long hop from Barnes was almost unprecedented. Hopwood was sure, by the sardonic look on Barnes's face, that the delivery was no accident.

During Barnes's early days as professional in the Lancashire League, he was at Old Trafford when the county played a League side which comprised 13 amateurs and two professionals. A. N. Hornby was captain of Lancashire and when he looked at the League team he said the two professionals were of no use to the county and asked if there were any young professionals. He was told of Barnes's presence and Hornby said to him: "We want you to play in this match because we are on the lookout for young players who will be some use to the county." Barnes refused to play, saying that if he could not be chosen in the first place, he would feel like a makeshift. He did agree to go to the ground for a trial and told Hornby what he was earning. Hornby said they would want three men for that and there was a suggestion of putting Barnes in the second team. Barnes was having none of that. "I don't want to boast," he said, "but I think I am as good as half your first eleven as it is." That finished thoughts of playing for Lancashire for a time. But the county returned, Barnes played in a couple of games in 1899, and two years later went with MacLaren to Australia.

Barnes had only two seasons on Lancashire's groundstaff and his best was his last, in 1903, when he was aged 30 and took 131 wickets at 17.85 runs each. He explained later that he left because the club would not find him winter work or agree to him having the match against Yorkshire for his benefit. So he returned to league cricket, although he was still good enough to tour

Barnes found the daily demands of county cricket too irksome.

SYDNEY BARNES

Australia twice more, and South Africa, and play in 23 more Test matches. He played in 27 Tests in all and returned the incredible figures of 189 wickets at the low average of 16.43 runs each. His 17 wickets for 159 runs in the match with South Africa at Johannesburg in 1913-14 — when he was 40 years old, incidentally — is second only to Jim Laker's 19 for 90 against Australia at Old Trafford in 1956. He took 49 wickets in four Tests in that series, at the remarkable average of 10.93 each.

Barnes himself regarded his best performance as being against Australia at Melbourne in 1911-12 when his opening spell gave him figures of 11-7-6-5. When Barnes was later booed for taking his time setting his field, he threw the ball to the ground, folded his arms and refused to bowl again until the barracking stopped. His uncertain temper and irascible nature often came to the surface, once even during a charity match in the 1930s when he was in his fifties. A galaxy of stars in the match included Learie Constantine, a great entertainer who found himself struggling for runs. Cec Parkin, realising that a bit of Constantine hitting was needed to entertain the crowd, turned to Barnes. "Chuck 'em to him, Syd," he said, "Let the crowd see him crack one or two." Barnes threw the ball down, collected his sweater from the umpire and refused to finish the over or bowl again in the match. As he put on his sweater, he turned to Parkin and said tersely: "I have a reputation as well as Constantine." His grumpiness and cussedness, however, left him over the years as he mellowed and began to seek the companionship he had spurned in his playing days. He died in Staffordshire on Boxing Day, 1967, aged 94.

WILLS'S CIGARETTES.

S. F. BARNES (STAFFORDSHIRE).

Barnes played the majority of his 27 Test Matches for England in Australia.

S. F. BARNES WARWICKSHIRE AND LANCASHIRE
BORN 19.4.1873, SMETHWICK, STAFFORDSHIRE

BATTING

	Matches	Innings	Not out	Runs	High score	Avg	100
Test	27	39	9	242	38*	8.06	0
First class	133	173	50	1,573	93	12.78	0

BOWLING AND FIELDING

	Runs	Wickets	Avg	5 W/I	10 W/M	BB	Ct	St
Test	3,106	189	16.43	24	7	9/103	12	0
First class	12,289	719	17.09	68	18	9/103	72	0

cricket heroes

KEN BARRINGTON

Michael Henderson

The loss to English cricket of Ken Barrington, who died of a heart attack during the Bridgetown Test in March 1981, was more significant than the passing-away of a hardy old trooper. For, as Fortinbras said on Hamlet's death, he was likely, had he been put on, to have prov'd most royal.

Barrington, who was assistant manager in the Caribbean after fulfilling the same role in each of the previous two winter tours, was the best full-time manager England never had. He had the aptitude, experience and, most important, the players' respect. Had he lived, England need not have been as rudderless in the eighties.

How's this for prescience? "There should be a four-day match played in midweek on the best possible wickets. I reckon the combination of four days and fast wickets would produce cricket at its best. Young players would grow more accustomed to Test conditions, and styles and results would more fairly reflect the merits of opposing teams. The forced declarations and bun-fights that produce some of our present three-day results would be out." Those were Barrington's pointers in 1968, his 16th and final season with Surrey. The following spring, after suffering a heart attack in a Melbourne double-wicket competition, the Reading-born son of a soldier retired. 'The Colonel' had made 31,714 runs, 6,806 of them in Tests at an average (58.67) bettered only by Herbert Sutcliffe among English players.

He had earned his rites of passage. In an era lit up by May, Cowdrey and Graveney, then Dexter, Barrington supplied the ballast. His initial experience of Test cricket, against South Africa, in 1955, was not a success — he made a duck. Four years later he was recalled and could not be budged after his maiden century against West Indies in January 1960. "The perfect English professional," said Wally Grout, "efficient, rugged and full of guts." The title of his autobiography, *Playing It Straight*, was apt. When he was recommended to Surrey colts in 1948 it was as much for his leg-spin as his batting. Thereafter he never let his county down, nor his country, though he was dropped as a disciplinary measure, for slow scoring, in 1965. Honesty and loyalty were the leitmotifs of his service.

At times, perhaps, he was too honest. He accused Charlie Griffith of

Ken Barrington and John Edrich acknowledge the applause of the Headingley crowd and the New Zealand team during the third Test in 1965.

c r i c k e t   h e r o e s

KEN BARRINGTON

chucking in 1963, and refused to play against West Indies the following summer for an England XI in exhibition matches at Edgbaston and Lord's. In November 1966 MCC sent a questionnaire to all capped players: Do you enjoy playing county cricket? Only seven said 'no' and one of them was Barrington. He didn't object to hard work but it had become relentless.

Honesty, loyalty. Those qualities were absorbed as a young professional in the Surrey side which won seven successive championships under Stuart Surridge and Peter May. Possibly it was the best-balanced of all champion sides. Certainly it was strong enough for Barrington to be dropped in 1958 during his transition from young dasher to responsible accumulator.

Vincit qui patitur: he who endures, conquers. The motto was slipped to Barrington by his wife, Ann, in 1964 when his endurance had been notable for a decade. Oddly enough he had not until then made a Test century in England. After making nine overseas, he amassed 256 in eleven and a half hours against Australia at Old Trafford. It remains the highest English Test innings at Manchester.

Why the outstanding foreign record? On his admission Barrington, of the two-eyed stance, shifted his priorities after his early exposure. He became a back-foot player, a hooker and cutter, who excelled on firmer, faster pitches. Of his 20 Test centuries, 14 were abroad. He made centuries in every Test-playing country, and on each Test ground in England.

Hundreds were not always enough in those days, when England were expected to beat the emerging nations at will. The selectors were not at all pleased by Barrington's 137 against New Zealand at Edgbaston in 1965, ground out in seven and a half hours at a time when he was out of form. His response to being dropped was a 'good luck' telegram to Peter Parfitt, who replaced him, and, on his recall for Headingley, an innings of 163 in a partnership of 369 with John Edrich, a triple centurion.

It would be wrong to mark him down as a mere occupier of the crease. Barrington enjoyed a fine sense of occasion, three times posting a Test century with a six. On the last of these inspired moments, at Melbourne in 1966, his carefree 115 was a veritable throwback. But usually the cap fitted, and he wore it without complaint even if, as once happened at Old Trafford, spectators lowered the pavilion flag during the Surrey innings, bored by his defiance.

c r i c k e t   h e r o e s

KEN BARRINGTON

His record against Australia was outstanding — 2,111 runs at 63.96, a higher average than any batsman on either side except Bradman and Sutcliffe. His aggregate of 1,451 on MCC's 1962/3 tour (Test average 72.75) has been bettered only by Hammond. Nor was he a negligible bowler. His 29 Test wickets included Sobers, Nurse, Hunte and Walcott. By the time illness forced him into early retirement — and he remained good enough to make 143 at Port of Spain in 1968 — Barrington had come a long way from the youth who started on £2 10s a week 20 years before. Between 1975 and 1980 he was a Test selector, in which time he managed the last two tours under MCC colours.

He had more to offer, for he was an uncomplicated man, happy to work in the nets with 'the boys,' a helpful, never obstructive, presence. Pleasingly his name lives on at the Oval, in the new construction due for completion in time for the 1990 season.

K. F. BARRINGTON SURREY
BORN 24.11.30, READING, BERKSHIRE

BATTING

	Matches	Innings	Not out	Runs	High score	Avg	100
Test	82	131	15	6,806	256	58.67	20
First class	533	831	136	31,714	256	45.63	76

BOWLING AND FIELDING

	Runs	Wickets	Avg	5 W/I	10 W/M	BB	Ct	St
Test	1,300	29	44.82	0	0	3/4	58	0
First class	8,907	273	32.62	8	0	7/40	515	0

Barrington lashes out at a ball during the second Test against Pakistan in 1967.

ALEC BEDSER

Trevor Bailey

Alec Bedser was the best post-war fast medium bowler. His nearest rivals would probably be Ian Botham, in Test — though not in county — matches, and Terry Alderman, who has demonstrated so successfully on his two England tours the value of bowling straight, and that it is still possible to take a large number of wickets in Test cricket without being genuinely quick. On all pitches and in all conditions I would place Alec ahead of both Ian and Terry, and alongside the pre-war Maurice Tate, though Alec was more deadly than the great Sussex bowler on wet and dusty wickets — in fact only just behind the legendary S. F. Barnes, surely the greatest bowler in the history of the game.

I first encountered Alec in war-time charity matches, but did not really know him and his other half, Eric, until the immediate post-war period, when he quickly established himself as the top new ball bowler in the country. In those days the 'Big Fella' was an honest workman — still learning to perfect his trade because of those five years in the RAF — who relied mainly on late in-swing, superb control and a very big heart. The last quality was essential, as in the early part of his Test career he frequently had to carry the attack on his broad shoulders. This was especially true during the 1946-47 Australian tour when, with only one other bowler of international calibre in the England party, Doug Wright, he simply soldiered on for hour after hour, duplicating as both shock and stock bowler against a world class batting line-up on good batting pitches.

Alec reached his peak in the early fifties, by which time he had become the complete artist, an absolute master of his craft. In addition to accuracy, late swing and stamina, he had acquired several other skills. He had learned how to push the ball away from the right hander, as distinct from swerving the ball. Rather strangely, his natural inswing was the product of a near-perfect, classical body action designed for an away swinger. He had a well-disguised slower ball and possessed the most devastating leg-cutter I have ever seen.

The reason why Alec's leg-cutter was so devastating stemmed from the size and strength of his fingers. The tips of my fingers, quite apart from being much more delicate, only just reached the first knuckle of his, which meant that he could spin his leg-cutter with the knowledge that on a wet or dusty pitch it would virtually always turn sharply, whereas most bowlers hope their leg-cut

c r i c k e t   h e r o e s

ALEC BEDSER

will bite after pitching. In addition, his leg-cutter was bowled at the same pace as his standard delivery and, unlike so many, could not be picked from the action. On one occasion I watched from the other end as he bowled five consecutive balls at Doug Insole on a helpful pitch at the Oval. All five dipped in, pitched leg and went over the top of the off stump without Doug being able to make contact. The sixth took the edge and went through the slips at catchable height to the boundary. Alec's comment upon this injustice was typical: "I always thought you were a lucky so and so, and now I've proved it."

Although I had shared the new ball with Alec for England against New Zealand in 1949, it was not until the 1950-51 tour to Australia I fully realised that my partner was not just a very fine bowler, but unquestionably a great one. My pace was lively, as distinct from quick, but I wanted my wicket-keeper standing back, because it increased the catching area behind the stumps, while Alec preferred him to be standing up, using him almost as a target. He was fortunate to have, in Godfrey Evans and Arthur MacIntyre, two outstanding performers, but even more important, he seldom strayed off line. In the slips and the gulley I was able to admire and study a high quality seamer at work. In the five Australian Tests on the 1950-51 tour, he captured 30 wickets at 16 apiece against a powerful batting line-up, and, apart from one innings, on plumb wickets.

In the next series, in England in 1953, when he was at the height of his powers, his haul was 39 at 17 apiece. His bowling in both innings of the first Test at Trent Bridge constituted the finest controlled display of fast medium bowling I have ever witnessed. The figures speak for themselves — 38.3/16/55/7 out of a total of 249, including dismissing Lindsay Hassett after he had scored a hundred with a ball which swung in late, pitched middle and leg and just clipped the off stump, and in the second innings 17.2/7/44/7 out of a total of 144. He sent down a total of 1,332.3 overs for his 162 wickets in first-class cricket that summer, illustrating his stamina and supporting his contention that the best practice for bowlers is bowling.

Batting against Alec was an intriguing experience. From the moment you took guard you felt enclosed, with the keeper breathing down your neck, two slips, a gulley and two backward short legs. His pace, about the same as that of Neil Foster, was sharp, but what increased the pressure, in addition to the

Another breakthrough for Bedser, comprehensively bowling Alderman of Derbyshire at the Oval in 1947.

ALEC BEDSER

probable movement in the air and off the pitch, were the few, very few, deliveries one could leave alone. I cannot recall a full toss, and half volleys were as rare as a truthful politician.

After that disastrous experiment of relying upon an all-seam attack in Brisbane, Alec was dropped for the second Test, which England won, and a typhoon called Tyson began to blow Australian batsmen away. It sadly signalled the end of his distinguished international career in which he took 236 wickets in 51 Tests. Ironically the conditions in Sydney were tailor-made for the 'Big Fella', as it was one of the few occasions when I relied on swing rather than movement off the seam, and I am convinced he would have captured at least six wickets in the first innings and therefore remained in the side for at least the next two Tests.

Alec continued to play for Surrey, for whom he took 1,459 wickets at 19 apiece, until 1960, but that was not to be the end of his long association with international and county cricket, which meant so much to him. He went on to become England's longest-serving selector, was Chairman from 1969 to 1981, managed England on several overseas tours, and was President of Surrey. A sound and sensible selector (unpaid, of course), Alec did experience some difficulty in coming to terms with standards which were different from those he had been brought up on, while at times he was a little short of imagination. He must wonder these days at the considerable sums of money now being paid to a number of individuals for doing the job which he did for nothing, for so long, and far more successfully.

An example of the flowing Bedser style.

A. V. BEDSER SURREY
BORN 4.7.18, READING, BERKSHIRE

BATTING

	Matches	Innings	Not out	Runs	High score	Avg	100
Test	51	71	15	714	79	12.75	0
First class	485	576	181	5,735	126	14.51	1

BOWLING AND FIELDING

	Runs	Wickets	Avg	5 W/I	10 W/M	BB	Ct	St
Test	5,876	236	24.89	15	5	7/44	26	0
First class	39,279	1,924	20.41	96	16	8/18	289	0

c r i c k e t h e r o e s

IAN BOTHAM

Alan Lee

Very few sportsmen have been the subject of *This is Your Life* at the age of 25. But then very few sportsmen bear comparison with Ian Botham. He would have been a titan purely on the strength of his cricketing deeds, but his lifestyle and personality have promoted him to the foreground of the nation's celebrities. Like so many of this elite breed, he may not universally be loved but he can never be ignored.

The first thing a person learns, on coming into close contact with Ian Terence Botham, is that he is a relentless competitor. He is not happy unless he has a challenge in sight, however trivial or diverse. The second thing a person learns is that Botham expects to win. It is this indomitable optimism which has marked every phase of his cricketing life, from the time he boldly announced to England's Centenary Test side in 1977 that he would soon be taking one of their places (he did) to the time, 11 years on, when he poured scorn on those who believed that a serious back injury would finish him (it did not).

Between times, he has broken more records than I would care to recount. He has won matches which seemed irretrievably lost and he has learned to fly a plane, play baseball, drive racing cars and own racehorses. He can resemble the old-style country gentleman with his pursuits of fishing and shooting, he can hold a lucid conversation on everything from politics to medical science and he has raised many thousands of pounds for leukaemia research.

Oh yes, he has also raised hell. Quite frequently, actually. The darker, undisciplined side of his character has not always been endearing, even if some of the stories about him have been the products of either a fanciful imagination or a mischief bordering on malice. He has, and I think he would admit this much, sometimes relied on the goodwill and good nature of others to extract him from scrapes. But equally, he has never gone short of that goodwill because Botham has attracted friends of influence and importance through sheer weight of personality. On his good days, and they greatly outnumber his bad ones, he is gregarious, generous and hugely amusing. If he has sometimes surrounded himself with characters who do him little credit, this is the habitual penance of the champion sportsman, and, to date, he has always kept them under control rather than, as in some sad cases, vice-versa.

A young Ian Botham reels after being hit by a ball from Andy Roberts during a Benson and Hedges cup tie in 1974. After spitting out two teeth, he recovered to play a match-winning innings for Somerset.

c r i c k e t   h e r o e s

IAN BOTHAM

He would probably tell you, if you were to quiz him about his greatest sporting memory, that it was not Headingley 1981 nor Bombay 1980 but a football match he played for Scunthorpe United at Bournemouth around the same time. This sums him up, for he has never been content to luxuriate in the plaudits for his cricketing heroics. Instead he has constantly sought new horizons. Had he set out to make a career in professional football he would doubtless have made a success of it, but the loss to cricket would have been incalculable.

Back in the Worcester attack after many had written him off — always a foolish thing to do — after a serious back injury.

He was born in Cheshire in 1955 but his family soon moved to Yeovil and, after a spell on the MCC groundstaff, he naturally joined Somerset in 1974. Although raw, his talent was quickly evident and the 1976 *Wisden* records: "Botham continued his development as a useful seam bowler of increasing pace, while his brilliant fielding and batting laden with potential make him a great asset." Somerset's captain at the time was Brian Close and if the rebellious young Botham was to concede respect to any elder it was to Close, a vigorous disciplinarian who believed in leading by example. Even now, when asked to nominate which cricketers he learned from, Close is the first name mentioned by Botham.

He came into the England side against the raggle-taggle 1977 Australians, a team ravaged and divided by the pickings of Kerry Packer. On his debut, Botham took five for 74 at Nottingham; in the next game at Leeds he took five for 21. England won both matches and a legend was born. England, remarkably, won 14 of the first 18 Tests in which Botham was included. At the end of that period, he had scored three centuries and taken five or more wickets in an innings no fewer than nine times

The best, though, was yet to come. In the spring of 1980 England stopped over at Bombay on their way home from Australia. They played one Test and seldom can a game at the highest level have been so utterly monopolised by one man. Botham scored 114 in his only innings and took 13 wickets. It was his

c r i c k e t   h e r o e s

IAN BOTHAM

last match before being made England captain in succession to his guru, Mike Brearley. This, however, was not a period he remembers with any affection. He was obliged to lead two consecutive series against the formidable West Indies. England lost them both, though not disastrously, but the suspicion grew that his own irreplaceable playing talents were being impaired by responsibility. After making a 'pair' in the second Test of the 1981 series against Australia, Botham resigned, only to be told he would have been sacked anyway.

What happened next is chronicled as well as any dramatic passage in the game's history. England, one down with four to play, recalled Brearley as captain and won the next three Tests to take the Ashes. Botham's centuries, at Headingley and Old Trafford, were unforgettable; so too, his decisive bowling spell of five wickets for one run on a Sunday of high summer and even higher excitement at Edgbaston.

It is fatuous to complain that Botham has not touched such heights again. Has anyone in the annals of the game ever taken a series so firmly in hand — especially one that had begun in such personal distress ? There was, too, a good deal still in store, including the fastest-ever double-century in Test cricket, taken off the 1982 Indians and, two years on, his fifth instance of a century and five wickets in the same match. No other Test player has achieved this more than twice, a significant measure of the man's greatness.

Even in his mid-30s he hits harder and catches better than almost anyone. Written off many times, Botham refuses to go quietly. All through life, he has been the same.

On his way to a century during the remarkable Headingley Test against the Australians in 1981.

I. T. BOTHAM SOMERSET AND WORCESTERSHIRE
BORN 24.11.55, HESWALL, CHESHIRE

BATTING

	Matches	Innings	Not out	Runs	High score	Avg	100
Test	97	154	5	5,119	208	34.35	14
First class	346	533	38	16,841	228	34.02	33

BOWLING AND FIELDING

	Runs	Wickets	Avg	5 W/I	10 W/M	BB	Ct	St
Test	10,633	376	28.27	27	4	8/34	112	0
First class	28,397	1,061	26.76	56	8	8/34	317	0

c r i c k e t   h e r o e s

GEOFFREY BOYCOTT

Michael Henderson

In the post-war years which belong to that most peculiar period, the recent past, a shy young man was growing up in the Yorkshire coalfield. He was a dedicated amateur cricketer and, though not overburdened with natural gifts, was eager to swap his clerk's job in the Ministry of Pensions for a professional career.

Early indications were not promising. Although members of his family had chipped into a kitty on his 11th birthday, to provide coaching at an indoor nets, recognition came slowly. The Yorkshire School was then the hardest. An adolescent's aptitude for hard work, by itself, impressed no-one. As he approached manhood, others, less keen, won better notices. It hurt. He gave up the clerk's job in order to practise, practise, practise. To and fro he went, from Barnsley to Leeds, an independent soul burning with purpose.

In time coaches came to admire his single-mindedness but he was far from fulfilled. Peers continued to advance, some of them from posh schools. Philip Sharpe, one such chap, did not practise four times a day, yet he was a Yorkshire first-teamer and, in 1962, was named Young Cricketer of the Year.

The bespectacled civil servant came of age the following season. He made his first championship century against Lancashire at Bramall Lane and went on to emulate Sharpe's achievement. In 1964 he won Test selection against South Africa; the next summer ended with a century in the Gillette Cup final. Old-timers were agreed, a formidable opening batsman had arrived.

By now this singular man, who spurned ale and horseplay, had earned the respect of the Yorkshire dressing room. Brian Close was still captain, Fred Trueman was charging in from the Kirkstall Lane End. There were no duffers: Illingworth, Padgett, Taylor, Binks, Wilson, Hampshire, Nicholson, Sharpe. They were heady days! From 1966 to 1968 Yorkshire won three successive championships. Yet there was unease, if not unrest, beneath the surface. Trueman retired, Close went to Somerset and Illingworth to Leicester. The gauche miner's son became, through his claim to a regular England spot, the senior pro.

He was dropped from the Test side in 1967 for slow scoring, when the selectors considered an unbeaten innings of 246 against India at Headingley to

Geoff Boycott returned to the England team after his three years of self-imposed exile and went on to score more runs for his country than any other batsman.

GEOFFREY BOYCOTT

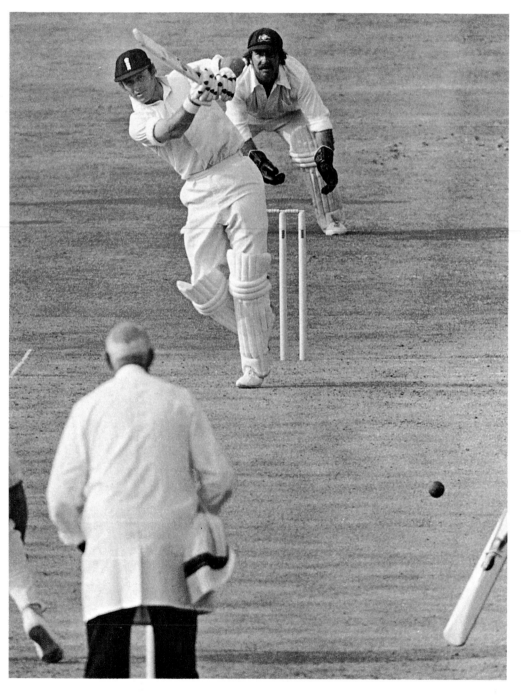

The stroke which took Boycott to his century of centuries, against the Australians at Headingley in 1977.

be just too non troppo. But on the whole these were fruitful summers: runs, fame, acclaim.

The seasons of 1970 and 1971 were especially good. In the first year of the new decade he plundered 2,051 runs. Together with John Edrich he was one of the twin batting pillars on which Illingworth's England side contested, and won, that winter's rubber in Australia. The series set a famous year in motion. The established opener made 1,535 runs in Australia, 657 of them in five Tests. Then, returning to Yorkshire as the new county captain — still run-drunk — 2,503 more, including 13 centuries, propelled him into the record books as the first player to average more than 100 in a championship season. Eight years later, relieved of the captaincy, he was to repeat the feat.

For all his qualities, captaincy proved an elusive skill. The dedicated professional, who could count to six and judge which of two ends was safer to run to, was never equipped for collaboration. Yorkshire had good players but the team was no longer successful. Members looked covetously towards Leicester and Taunton where their exiles had put down firm roots.

"Good morning, gentlemen," a team-mate would announce each morning, pausing to add: "Good morning, Boycott." That the colleague's surname was Hutton, the public school-educated son of the man who cast the longest shadow over Yorkshire batting, must have pained him. Embattled, soon to become embittered, the captain could not bend all men to his will.

Nor would the world pay him his due. To John Arlott he was a 'lonely perfectionist', to Neville Cardus an 'honest artisan'. No moon in June romance there. "Bowling to him has always been a mixed emotion," wrote Mike Selvey, a member of the Middlesex side which won three championship titles outright and shared another under Mike Brearley. "With the elation of beating the best defence in the world goes the knowledge that in spite of his relentlessness the fielding side always has one end under control."

Frustrated by his inability to arrest Yorkshire's decline, overlooked for the England captaincy when Illingworth was chopped, the man of moods proved unable to curb his resentment. For three long years, during which English batsmen were pummelled by Lillee and Thomson in two continents, and wounded by Michael Holding at his fastest, the Test side was deprived of its straightest bat. When his selfishness was most needed, he was not there.

Bat held aloft, Boycott acknowledges the applause as his home supporters acclaim his 100th century.

c r i c k e t   h e r o e s

GEOFFREY BOYCOTT

Let cricket lovers debate why. When the Yorkshire Achilles eventually stirred from his tent in 1977, an England side which had taken so much punishment from Australia was returning fire. Lillee was absent but Thomson was around. The masterly defensive opener ground out a century on his Test return at Trent Bridge and another, his 100th, at Headingley. In the jubilant afterglow he talked of "my public." Sunset Boulevard had come to the West Riding.

Otherwise affairs at Headingley were unhappy. The relationship between the Grand Old Man and his team-mates became so sour that he was sacked as captain in 1978, and Illingworth was recalled from Leicester. As Illingworth had built a side at Grace Road good enough to win its first championship, and collect four one-day pots, hopes at Yorkshire were high. The native soil was less fertile. Illingworth was confronted by a personality cult around the venerable, and venerated, batsman so strong that normal social intercourse was at times impossible. In their own way, John Hampshire, Chris Old and Bill Athey decided they had had enough, and left.

In the England side the 40-year-old was invigorated by younger men. He led the side briefly, and unsuccessfully, in New Zealand, when Brearley was injured. On Brearley's return in 1981, he again belonged to an England side which regained the Ashes. The last of his 22 Test centuries came against Lillee and Alderman at The Oval. Six months later a Test career which spanned 18 years was over. The circumstances of departure were messy: a valedictory note left on a corkscrew in the dressing room. He was sent home. After 108 Tests and 8,114 runs (then a world record) his time was up. Later that spring he turned up in South Africa, playing for beer (or, in his case, ginseng) money.

Controversy remained a loyal companion. In 1983 he was sacked by Yorkshire yet swam back on a tidal wave of public support not only with a new contract but also as the Wakefield representative of the reconstituted club committee. At an extraordinary meeting in Harrogate the self-styled Reform Group routed the old guard.

His 1984 testimonial produced a club record, £148,000. The following year he scored his 100th century for Yorkshire; the year after, his 150th first-class century. He ended the season eight runs short of 1,000, the first time he had failed to reach that landmark since 1962. It was his final fling; on September 23rd he was sacked, this time for good.

cricket heroes

GEOFFREY BOYCOTT

Things ended painlessly. He was thanked for his efforts by a cricket committee he despised, and on which he has never subsequently served despite offers. For fully 15 months after his dethronement, a year in which Yorkshire won the Benson and Hedges Cup, the Wakefield representative absented himself from club business.

Naturally there was a record to put straight, which he attempted to do in an autobiography, less well-written and certainly less convincing than the book on him by Don Mosey, a one-time acquaintance who was eventually designated a non-person. He prefaced his own book with a line of Thoreau's about marching to different drums. Others suggested Shelley: "Look on my works, ye mighty, and despair".

In his 50th year what can he reflect on? A working life which brought fame and infamy; more runs for England than anyone; more Test centuries than anyone except Hammond and Cowdrey; the support of admirers and the respect of opponents; the passing into popular folklore. Does he now, rich beyond expectation, glimpse, through the post-war mist, the 10-year-old lad who won a Len Hutton bat in a local newspaper competition? How pleased that schoolboy must have been, the world so wonderful and so much to conquer.

Was he free? Was he happy? The question is absurd:

Had anything been wrong we should certainly have heard.

A rare sight as Boycott bowls for England against West Indies.

G. BOYCOTT YORKSHIRE
BORN 21.10.40, FITZWILLIAM, YORKSHIRE

BATTING

	Matches	Innings	Not out	Runs	High score	Avg	100
Test	108	193	23	8,114	246*	47.72	22
First class	609	1,014	162	48,426	261*	56.83	151

BOWLING AND FIELDING

	Runs	Wickets	Avg	5 W/I	10 W/M	BB	Ct	St
Test	382	7	54.57	0	0	3/47	33	0
First class	1,459	45	32.42	0	0	4/14	264	0

MIKE BREARLEY

Scyld Berry

*Mike Brearley —
England's most astute
captain?*

Since no one person has watched over a hundred years of Test cricket, it is impossible to say definitively that so-and-so was the finest captain that England has had. But I will argue that Mike Brearley has been as good as any. In two home series against Australia, in 1977 and 1981, he won three Tests and did not lose one himself. In fact, when Brearley was captain, England went three whole summers without a defeat, quite the reverse of recent years when every Allan, Viv and Imran has won a series in England. If a grey-bearded, silver-haired figure with sloping shoulders stood at first slip and directed the national fortunes, cricket followers could be sure that England would not fail for want of thought.

One must, however, have reservations about every cricketer, because no human being can deal perfectly with every facet of such an intricate game. In Brearley's case, they do not really concern his captaincy, and in only a small measure his batting, although that could be a cause of anxiety — in 1978 for example. Rather, these reservations concern his merits as a selector while England captain, but even these did not arise until the later stages of his career.

Perhaps the wisest move that 'Gubby' Allen made was to back Brearley to cleanse the Middlesex stables, starting in the 1971 season. Brearley had been an outstanding batsman at Cambridge until 1964, scoring over 4,000 runs in four seasons there, but thereafter he had not made as many for Middlesex. He did not play a full season while he was furthering his philosophy in California or lecturing at Newcastle University. The challenge of being a leader, and of purging Middlesex of its discordant characters, was required to tempt him to become a full-time professional.

By 1976 he was established in the 1500 runs-a-year category, and chosen for the England side on batting merit. Against the West Indian fast bowlers, in two Tests that summer, he defended soundly enough to make one think that he was being saved for higher things when he was omitted. Sure enough, he was appointed Tony Greig's vice-captain in India and Australia that winter; and he established himself as an opening batsman, seen to best advantage when wearing the hair shirt of dogged defence — Geoff Boycott then was still in his tent — while a strokeplayer kept the scoreboard moving at the other end.

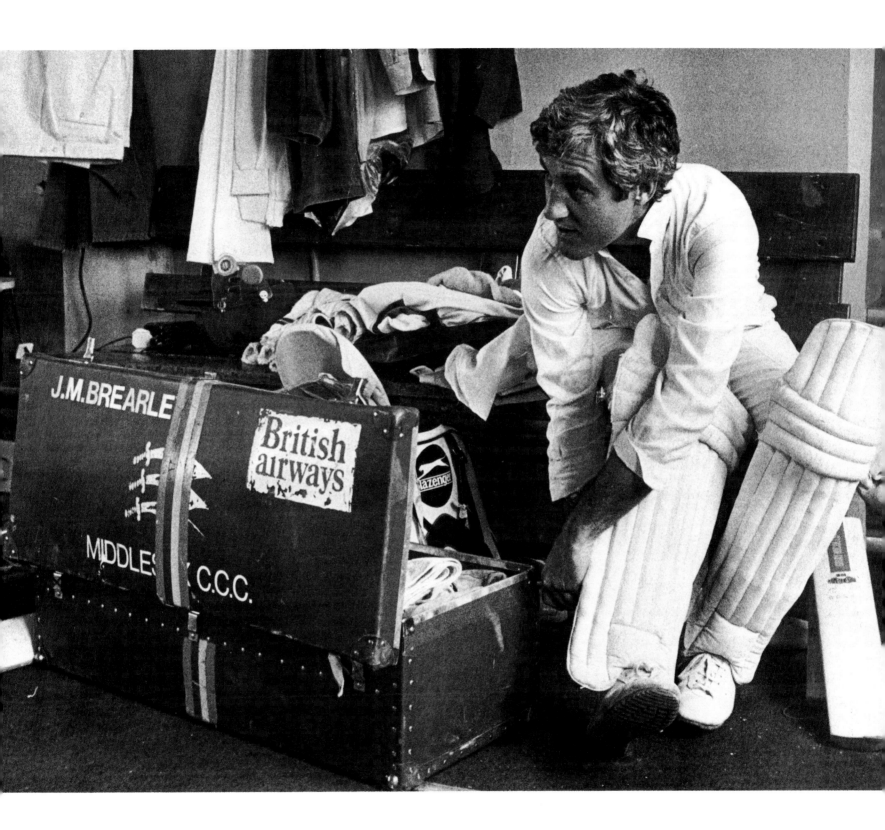

MIKE BREARLEY

Further elevation came more rapidly than anyone could have expected, when Greig used his position as England captain to get a good deal out of World Series Cricket. But Brearley was already prepared for the job, and for Greg Chappell's Australians. It was not until the Second Test that he made a questionable field-placing, by missing out a third slip for Doug Walters — and that mistake was quickly rectified, then far outweighed by his decision to persuade Derek Underwood to bowl over the wicket from the Stretford End. In the Third Test a bumptious lad announced himself with five wickets in an innings, and again in the following Test. Brearley's initial reaction to Ian Botham was far from favourable, as was the younger man's to Brearley. But when Brearley revealed the iron will beneath the exterior, he commanded the respect of his new match-winner.

Brearley throws the ball to Bob Willis, who was to play a major part in Brearley's triumph as England captain — three summers without defeat.

In those days a sporting club in London offered a case of champagne to the journalist who guessed aright the name of the first England batsman to make a century in each series. When England went off to Pakistan in 1977-8, Brearley was my nomination. He had batted well in the sub-continent before, even if he had not scored all of the 312 runs with which he was credited at Peshawar on England's Under-25 tour (one of the two local scorers walked out, and the other hadn't a clue which visitor was which). He was also a fine player of leg-spin, to which his square-driving was well suited.

So it came to pass that Brearley had an excellent chance to make his Test century in the Second Test at Hyderabad, Sind, when England had to bat out the last day against Abdul Qadir. By tea England had not lost a single wicket, Brearley's score was in the late sixties, Boycott's a little behind, and Pakistan were resigned to a draw. Here, then, was the ideal moment for the captain to unwind, play a few strokes and reach his landmark — and to refresh those parts of Pakistan where champagne did not otherwise reach. But no; he slowed down after tea, pottered around and then got out, while Boycott went on purposefully to his century, and even claimed the extra half-hour to do so! Brearley explained afterwards: "I became obsessed with the concept of the purity inherent in being not out." And I had to admire his candour in admitting to such complicated thoughts.

Being unable to modify his concentration from stern to relaxed prevented him batting fluently at Test level, but it was his strength as a captain. His best innings for England after 1978, when he struggled with the effects of a broken forearm and experimented with a helmet and a Greig-style backlift, were the rearguard actions at Perth and Melbourne in 1979-80 and at the Oval in 1981. He was batting down the order by then at number six or seven: in effect an all-rounder, not a batsman/bowler but a batsman/captain.

His defect, in my estimation, was that he was too conservative as a selector through being too loyal to his established players. During the World Series years this did not matter: Australia and Pakistan were enfeebled, almost Second XIs; India and New Zealand were gobbled up by Botham for breakfast. The warning signs came in the summer of 1979. Over the following two years England had to face a reunited Australia and West Indies each summer and winter: nothing but the toughest. And against such bowling it was obvious that England's existing batting would be too weak, with Brearley as one of five specialist batsmen, followed by Botham at six and Geoff Miller at seven, plus Bob Taylor and the bowlers. Therefore, if anyone was to be blooded for the fray to come, it had to be that summer when the going against India was easier. As it was, the 1979 series was not used for experiment as it might have been. Worse still perhaps, a dressing-room atmosphere was created that became hostile to change and outside interference. The positive aspect of team spirit was healthy; but not the antipathy towards the press, as it later grew to become paranoia, and certainly not the increasing antipathy towards former players, since it cut the new generation off from accumulated folk-wisdom.

When the changes came, they had to be made too suddenly. In the First Test of 1979-80 at Perth, Derek Randall opened, Peter Willey batted at number three, and Miller at five. They scored 55 runs between them, while Graham Gooch, who would have strengthened the medium-pace and the slip-fielding, was dropped after scoring two 50s in his previous state game. In that three-Test series England never got on to an equal footing and were almost carried

The successful summer of 1981 and Brearley discusses tactics with Botham at Edgbaston.

MIKE BREARLEY

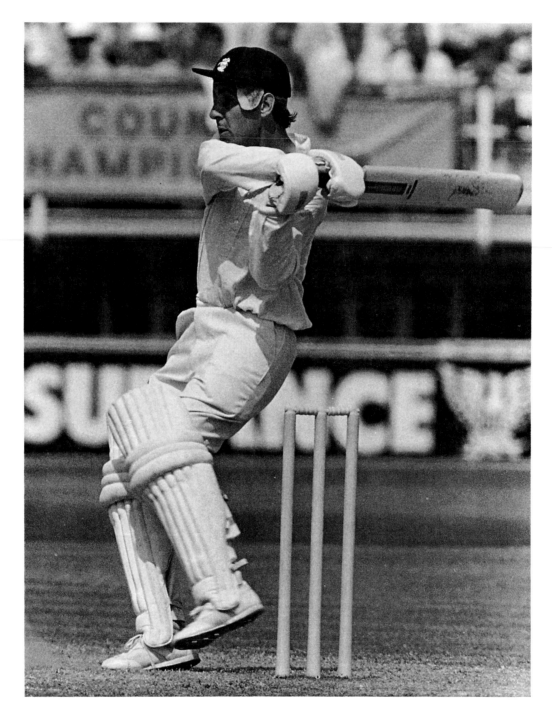

An atypical attacking stroke from Brearley; during the absence of Geoff Boycott Brearley's batting role was that of anchorman, allowing the stroke-players free reign at the other end.

MIKE BREARLEY

by Botham. Brearley handed over the captaincy to him, to resume it in 1981 for the oft-told climax of both of their careers.

By missing the Test matches against West Indies during Botham's interregnum, Brearley never led England against the unofficial world champions, which was a shame for students of the game. It would have been fascinating watching him trying to impose control on batsmen rampant. He always insisted on picking a full hand of bowlers so that he could maintain as much control as possible in the field. But would he have been able to do so on a belter at Lord's in 1973, when Kanhai, Sobers and Julien all hit centuries in spite of everything Arnold, Willis, Greig, Underwood and Illingworth himself could do?

For the rest, Brearley combined an eye for minute technical detail with the broad strategic vision required to plan a campaign, as only a handful of the finest skippers have done. He would, with almost visible relish, torture an opposing batsman with the sort of bowling he liked least, like off-spin for Australia's keeper MacLean in 1978-9. The same with his field placings: the field he set for Allan Border at Old Trafford in 1981, consisting of three close fielders and the rest around the boundary, when Australia had their last pair at the crease, was a Machiavellian masterpiece.

Anyone who has captained a cricket team must know there are occasions when the opposition goes on the rampage, the game slips away, and the mind is very tempted to go blank. In his wisdom, Brearley was able to prevent that happening during his Test career.

J. M. BREARLEY MIDDLESEX
BORN 28.4.42, HARROW, MIDDLESEX

BATTING

	Matches	Innings	Not out	Runs	High score	Avg	100
Test	39	66	3	1,442	91	22.88	0
First class	455	768	102	25,185	312*	37.81	45

BOWLING AND FIELDING

	Runs	Wickets	Avg	5 W/I	10 W/M	BB	Ct	St
Test	0	0	0	0	0	0	52	0
First class	192	3	64.00	0	0	1/6	418	0

BRIAN CLOSE

Don Mosey

When a man scores 34,994 runs, takes 1,171 wickets and holds 813 catches it is difficult to sustain an argument that he failed to live up to his youthful promise. When the same man leads England in seven Tests and does not lose any of them it seems impertinent to describe his Test career as unsuccessful. Yet that is almost certainly the judgment of history upon Dennis Brian Close — a man destined from the first to be a cricketing martyr.

When, in 1977, we embarked together on the writing of his life-story, I wanted to call it *The Slings and Arrows*, since it appeared to me that, throughout his career, outrageous fortune had attended his efforts more than those of many others less talented. Brian himself favoured the title *I Did it My Way*, not merely because of his fondness for the singing of Frank Sinatra but because he had recognised too late in life the subjectiveness of his approach. We finally settled on the publishers' compromise, *I Don't Bruise Easily*, which was magnificently ambiguous. Close was physically indestructible, the most courageous of batsmen and fieldsmen, but psychologically sensitive; when, in 1970, he was summoned to Headingley and given ten minutes by the Yorkshire cricket chairman, Brian Sellers, to resign or be sacked, he went away and was violently sick — literally so.

To those of us with close associations with league cricket in West Yorkshire the prodigious teenage talent of Brian Close was no secret. He had played his first league game at the age of eleven in the Airedale and Wharfedale League and quickly graduated to the toughest and most competitive single-innings cricket in the world, the Bradford League. At 18 he played his first game for Yorkshire's senior XI, along with a fast bowler who was just 18 days older — Freddie Trueman. By the end of that 1949 season Close had done the first-class double of 1,000 runs and 100 wickets and had made his debut for England. Within the next three years he had played football for Leeds United, Arsenal and Bradford City and become a category one golfer playing right-handed. Ten years later, on an impulse, he got rid of his clubs, bought a left-handed set and in less than a year he was once again a single-figure handicap player.

He was a gifted performer at squash, tennis, table tennis and snooker and excelled at any sort of party trick, particularly those requiring sheer strength,

BRIAN CLOSE

and when a mutual friend and I once took him to his first ever Rugby League match he borrowed a pair of boots at the end of the game and went out and kicked goals from all angles — the first time he had touched the oval-shaped ball. Close was probably the greatest all-round competitor I have ever known.

As a captain, he led from the front, ever ready to place himself in the most suicidal of positions close to the wicket whether the ball was turning or not. He had a flair which few before him or afterwards have ever possessed and could turn a game in a matter of seconds by an inspired switch of his bowlers or a change in the field. He was struck by the ball many times — on the side of the head, the forehead, the shin — but no one ever got him off the field. He remained there, blood pouring down his face or into his boot, snarling at his awestruck team to "Get on with it" because time was running out. These are not romantic flights of fancy, these things happened — against Surrey at Hull, against Gloucestershire at Harrogate, against Hampshire at Portsmouth, against Kent at Gravesend.

All-round sportsman and competitor Brian Close led Yorkshire to four Championships and two Gillette Cups in his eight years as captain.

He had the good captain's card-index mind of the strengths and weaknesses of all other players he encountered, in his own side as well as the opposition ranks. Bradman, Benaud and Hutton had this gift, Illingworth had it, Brearley had it and on the 1989 Australian tour to England we saw that Border had it too — or at any rate a combination of Border and his cricket manager, Bobby Simpson. Close's England side of 1966 at The Oval still talk about the way he 'conned' out the immortal Gary Sobers.

Close never talked players out by addressing them, rather by talking *about* them to close fielders. On this occasion he announced to his wicket-keeper John Murray, in Sobers's hearing, that he had instructed John Snow to bowl him a bouncer because: "Gary won't be able to resist trying to hook. If he mishits it on the offside he's yours, if he mishits it on the legside I've got him." Sobers couldn't believe what he was hearing. Snow duly followed Close's instructions, Sobers duly hooked and Close duly took the catch. Sobers walked off shaking his head in disbelief.

Close's personal contribution to that victory over the West Indies was four runs and no wickets, yet not one of his players could or would claim that he played a greater part in the success than the captain. In the following season he led England to five big wins and a rain-affected draw against India and

BRIAN CLOSE

Pakistan and was sacked for matters totally unconnected with Test cricket. In his eight years as county captain Yorkshire won the County Championship four times and the Gillette Cup twice, yet he was summarily dismissed.

The plain fact emerges that Close must have been one of the unluckiest cricketers ever. Misfortune and controversy dogged him at every step, each incident in a chequered career accompanied by massive publicity of an unwelcome nature. That is something which happens only to the hugely talented and/or the spectacular, larger-than-life characters of sport as his young friend (and to some extent his protege) Ian Botham was to discover.

That Close was a flawed sporting genius there can be no doubt. For all his 52 centuries, he never made a double hundred. His ability to analyse other players was brilliant but he could never come to terms with his own shortcomings. He had a masterly cricket brain, was (and is) an intelligent man, but showed on many occasions that he lacked simple common sense. He was the toughest of competitors on a sporting field of any kind but there was (and is) no malice in the man. That is why those who have known him all his life sometimes regard his cricket career as a tragedy rather than the triumph it promised to be when he did that first 'double' in 1949.

If that career did not in the end fulfil its earliest potential, Brian Close has at least left behind his philosophy of leadership which cannot in any way be faulted. "Captaincy," he once said, "is all about giving. You have to give something of yourself to every man you play with and all of yourself to the side."

D. B. CLOSE   YORKSHIRE AND SOMERESET
BORN 24.2.31, RAWDON, LEEDS, YORKSHIRE

BATTING

	Matches	Innings	Not out	Runs	High score	Avg	100
Test	22	37	2	887	70	25.34	—
First class	786	1,225	173	34,994	198	33.26	52

BOWLING AND FIELDING

	Runs	Wickets	Avg	5 W/I	10 W/M	BB	Ct	St
Test	532	18	29.55	0	0	4/35	24	0
First class	30,947	1,171	26.42	43	3	8/41	813	1

c   r   i   c   k   e   t   h   e   r   o   e   s

DENIS COMPTON

Jack Bailey

Denis Compton was the batting genius of his time. His talent was there for all to recognise, from the very young to the old wiseacres who had long since seen most of everything there was to see, and had been unimpressed by a great deal of that. His brand of batsmanship struck a chord in the same way that Robin Hood did, or Houdini, or Alexander the Great — instantly striking as in a class beyond compare.

We aspiring young cricketers in the late Forties had, I believe, the best view of Denis. He was everything you ever wanted to be — tousled, enjoying a lark, yet the brightest star in a glittering firmament when the dark skies of the war were still a strong and sombre memory.

Playing at the Oval in 1947 for the Young Amateurs of Surrey during the school holiday, the day's play shortened by an early finish, some of us made our way by tube across London, hurrying through the crowds, past the ticket barriers and up and down escalators in the hope of seeing the great man in action during that most famous of all his seasons. It was late August and until then we had been able to follow his exploits only via radio commentary and the pages of the press.

Our brief visit to the free seats at the Nursery End was rewarded by an innings of heroic content and proportions. Middlesex were making a gallant attempt to score 397 runs in the fourth innings for victory. To do so they had to score at 90 runs an hour. The pitch assisted the Kent spinners, Doug Wright, Ray Dovey and Jack Davies, and Middlesex lost their first four wickets for 130 runs. But all this was forgotten as Compton unfurled every stroke in his unique repertoire, smashing into smithereens every semblance of good order in the Kent attack while careering to his thirteenth century of the season, persuading the ball to the boundary nineteen times, making in all 168 runs out of the Middlesex total of 321 and carrying his team within sight of an elusive victory.

This was the golden summer of Compton's eighteen centuries — six of them against the touring South Africans — and 3,816 runs, when the sun shone unremittingly and he broke and remoulded every record for an individual in an English season. It was the flip of a coin as to whose was the best recognised face in England — Compton's, which appeared large on every London

Compton strides out with Bill Edrich to bat for England. Opposite page: Compton leaves the field at Hastings in 1947 after having made his 17th century of the summer, thus beating Jack Hobbs's 16 centuries of 1925.

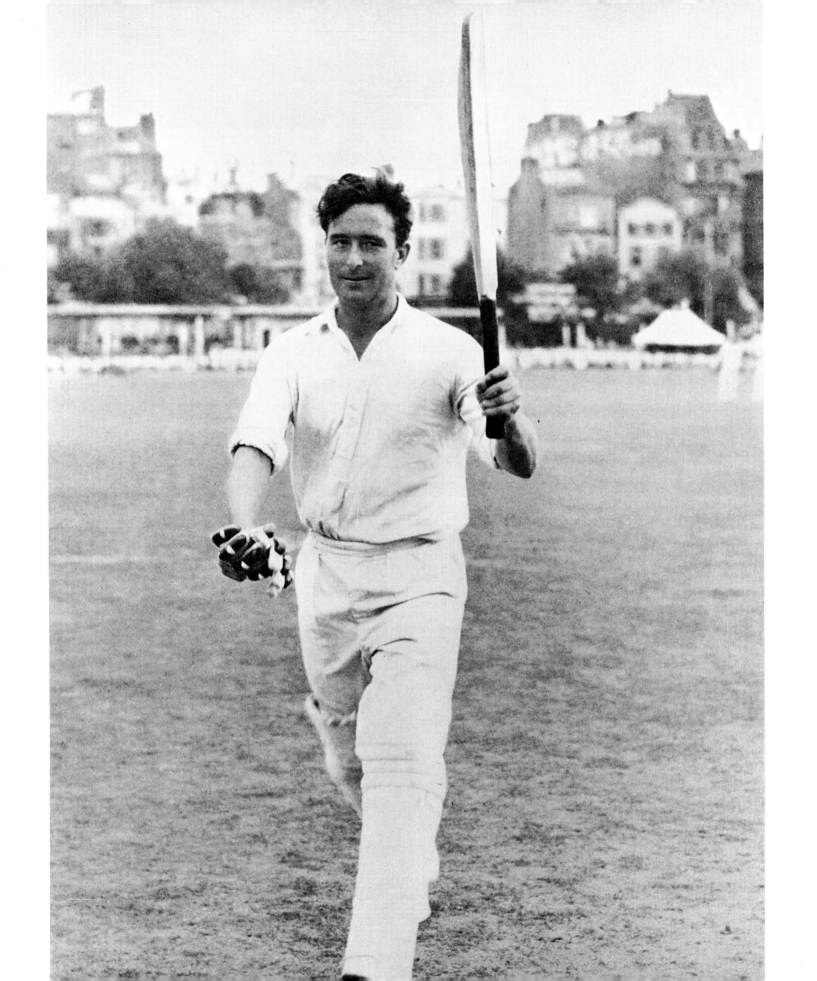

DENIS COMPTON

Transport bus promoting a well-known brand of hair cream, or Cary Grant's, or Winston Churchill's.

I was present when, a week or two later, he made 246 for the Champion County against the Rest at the Oval. Even now I can picture him advancing, tripping, falling and then sweeping Goddard off his nose from a virtually prone position, the ball going for four. It was then confirmed to all small boys what they had long suspected — that he was descended, like Superman, from some distant planet and was possessed of supernatural powers.

In fact, he was born in Hendon on 23rd May, 1918, the son of athletically-minded parents and brother of Leslie. Both brothers played football for Arsenal and England and cricket for Middlesex in the days when professional sportsmen were poorly rewarded financially and fun and good times were the spur.

Denis was 14 years old when he made 85 for North London Schools v South London Schools at Lord's. The following year, he scored 114 against a Public Schools team, again at Lord's — a ground he was to make largely his own. At the age of 17 he was already going in first wicket down for Middlesex. His debut for England came a year later. He had just turned 20 when he played his first innings against Australia and took his first century from the grudging hands of the old enemy.

He went on to a career, interrupted for five prime years by the war, which brought him 38,942 runs and 123 scores of more than a hundred. Nearly 6,000 of his runs came in Test matches. While 1947 was his most bountiful year, he had already outlined the shape of things to come when in 1946 he scored 2,403 runs, including ten centuries — two of them above 200.

That winter, in Australia, he joined the illustrious few who have made a century in each innings of a Test match. It was a series in which England failed to win a match, but it was also notable for the way in which Compton (like Edrich) reminded everyone that he was much more than a plunderer when the going was good. Now his batting included a large measure of courage and a refusal to be beaten by the best attack in the world — Lindwall and Miller high on the list.

Even as 1947 was coming to an end the injury to his knee, a result of his parallel life in football, had begun to trouble him. It was to become a

Anna Neagle, the actress, and Compton at the Empress Hall, London in 1949.

c r i c k e t   h e r o e s

DENIS COMPTON

progressively worrisome problem, restricting the movement up and down the wicket which was such an outstanding feature of his game. By 1949 it had grown worse, but it did not prevent him from taking South Africa by storm in 1948/9 when a prolific tour included 300 runs in as many minutes against N. E. Transvaal.

He was eventually to have a knee-cap removed and to fight a long and courageous battle against his disability, but until his last innings in the first class game in 1964 he remained a source of wonderment and joy to cricket followers the wide world over. He continued to play Test cricket until 1956/7 when even his marvellous relationship with South African Test matches and their crowds and cricketers had to come to an end.

His technique was always one which sought to establish a domination over the bowler so that the poor fellow became incapable of bowling line and length after Compton had been at the wicket a short time. He dictated the length at which the ball arrived with him by bewildering speed of foot. His ability to see the ball early and play it late and his powerful forearms and wrists enabled him constantly to improvise beyond the orthodoxy which was, make no mistake, at the heart of all his batting. The eternal schoolboy in him led to methods which in others would have been fatal — the sweep to whichever ball tickled his palate, the shimmy down the wicket to all but the fastest bowlers. His cover-driving left even the most defensive of fields standing by dint of his timing and his strong wrists. He also made powerful use of the cut and the hook, but seldom chose to play the straight drive, perhaps because it presented too little of a challenge.

Another four runs on the board as Compton keeps the scorers busy.

Challenge was always in the air when he was batting and he communicated his love of it instantly to the waiting, watching crowds. He was also a left-arm bowler of greater ability than he or his batting allowed fully to emerge and his fielding was capable of a brilliance possessed by few. One of life's rare talents, he was and is possessed of great friendliness and charm, instantly beguiling and never forgotten.

c r i c k e t   h e r o e s

DENIS COMPTON

Denis had his lean spells. In 1951/2 in Australia for instance, embattled by his knee, he had a wretched time. But he was possessed of great resilience. Even as late as 1963 it was much in evidence. Playing at Lord's for MCC against Pataudi's Oxford team, in front of a sparse crowd and out of practice, he made nought in the first innings. This followed scores of 0 and 1 in his previous two innings against the undergraduates. "They won't think I could ever bat," he told me.

The following day he arrived not before time, as had been known to happen before, borrowed somebody's bat and went out to do battle. For a time he was all at sea. Then it happened. "Come and watch this," called Charles Cobham from the dressing room balcony. We dropped everything and went to look. The Nawab was having difficulty in placing the field for his slow left arm bowler.

Faced with an offside field of six men, Denis had pierced the cordon three times in one over, once by the aerial route into the Mound Stand. Reinforcements were called up. Now the field was split seven/two. The next ball was pitched on the off-stump, of good length. It went, via the famous sweep, down to the very spot from whence the fielder had just been moved. They knew he could bat, all right.

"Some vague, unpunctual star... " wrote Rupert Brooke in a different context. But as an epitaph to Compton, the cricketer, it just about fits the bill.

Relaxing at home with one of the family pets in 1956, towards the end of an illustrious cricketing career.

D. C. S. COMPTON MIDDLESEX
BORN 23.5.18, HENDON, MIDDLESEX

BATTING

	Matches	Innings	Not out	Runs	High score	Avg	100
Test	78	131	15	5,807	278	50.06	17
First class	515	839	88	38,942	300	51.85	123

BOWLING AND FIELDING

	Runs	Wickets	Avg	5 W/I	10 W/M	BB	Ct	St
Test	1,410	25	56.40	1	0	5/70	49	0
First class	20,074	622	32.27	19	3	7/36	415	0

DENIS COMPTON

*"Some vague,
unpunctual star... "*

COLIN COWDREY

Ivo Tennant

Michael Colin Cowdrey's life was shaped as soon as he was born. His father, a tea planter whose passion for cricket was heightened by his regard for Marylebone Cricket Club, not only christened his son with its famous initials but, almost simultaneously, had him put down for membership. Had the boy become a golfer, or squash or rackets player — for he had no little talent at each — such a christening would have been seen as misguided, eccentric, even foolish; as it was, he became one of the best known, and best loved, of all cricketers.

In terms of statistics, by which he sets no great yardstick, he was one of England's finest batsmen. He played in more than 100 Test matches, scored more than 7,000 runs at an average of over 40 and scored a century of centuries. Such figures brook no argument; they distinguish him as a player of class from one who is merely proficient. Yet for some, colleagues and critics among them, this was not enough. Technically, they said, he was without peer and without fault; but he was too sensitive a person, too much of a theorist to destroy mediocre bowling. He batted well only when the situation demanded it, when there was a challenge to occupy his fertile mind.

Clearly there was truth in this, although it could be said he never appeared to be destroying bowling since he was not a batsman who had to hit the ball. Rather, he caressed it. Timing was everything. There are no pictures to be seen of Cowdrey executing murderous attacking shots in the manner of Sobers or Botham because he did not play them. Even in one-day cricket, which he did not care for, and which, fortunately for him, he did not have to suffer too often, he was loath to hit across the line.

Cowdrey was that phenomenon beloved by the media — a child prodigy. Even he could not explain the speed at which he developed as a cricketer to the extent that he was not let out of sight by his schoolmasters. He returned from India, his birthplace, at a young age to have the boarding school education that, for one of his middle class background, was taken for granted. The ethos of the prep and public schools he attended has not left him, nor the influence of their head masters. They were the earliest of several strong characters to make an impression upon his introspective being.

Cowdrey at the crease during his first tour of Australia in 1954-55.

c r i c k e t   h e r o e s

COLIN COWDREY

He was chosen for the 1st XI at Tonbridge just three weeks after arriving for his first term in 1946, when he was 13 years old. He was playing with boys for whom he was fagging. And he was out first ball. Even so, the young Cowdrey retained his place not only for the next match but for the climax to Tonbridge's season — their traditional encounter with Clifton at Lord's. Suffused with nerves, he scored 75 and 44 and realised then, if he had not before, that this was the game for him.

He made his first appearance for Kent when still a schoolboy, and his first for England when still at Oxford. It was obvious even to the most seasoned professional that Cowdrey possessed exceptional ability. At Scarborough in 1954 he made a century for Gentlemen against Players in the presence of Leonard Hutton, an innings which, more than any other, gained him a place on MCC's 1954-5 tour to Australia.

It was on that tour, the first of six which Cowdrey made to Australia, that he scored his first Test century. It was memorable not just for the fact that he made 102 out of a total of 191, but for the maturity with which the runs were made. This was not the innings of an undergraduate just turned 22; it was that of a craftsman. From then on it was clear that for as long as he cared to play cricket, Cowdrey would be an obvious choice for England.

If, then, his technique was as near to faultless as possible, why did he not score even more heavily than he did? There were certainly times when he pottered around the crease against bowlers who were hardly heard of again. His theorising and quest for new challenges could be attributed to his intellect; his inability or reluctance to realise just how good he was to innate modesty and the ethos of his upbringing. "The quiet style has always seemed to me to be the right way to carry one's talents," he wrote. He was the old-fashioned English gent who did not brag. There was, though, a further reason. His sensitivity was coupled with a tendency to worry which, combined with indecisiveness, were serious drawbacks.

Although he was fortunate with those who influenced or helped him — his father-in-law Stuart Chiesman became both chairman of Kent and his part-time employer — he was not the luckiest of cricketers. Of the 27 Tests in which he captained England, ten were against West Indies and Sobers in his prime. Because he was so manifestly gifted he would not only find the boundary while

COLIN COWDREY

others would play and miss but he would get an edge to a ball which others would not come close to touching. When the captaincy was his, seemingly for keeps, he snapped an achilles tendon in a Sunday slogabout. Illingworth, in many ways his complete opposite, deputised and remained as captain for the tour to Australia the following year, 1970.

Even after he retired, having been consigned in his last seasons to batting too low in the Kent order, his marital break-up received an inordinate amount of publicity. When he reached the summit of his cricketing career in becoming President of MCC he had to undergo a heart by-pass operation, the cause of which was, perhaps, not unrelated to his having to resolve differences between MCC and the Test and County Cricket Board which came to an ugly climax with the resignation of MCC's secretary and treasurer.

Yet it is for his felicitous stroke-play that Cowdrey will be best remembered. He made cricket appear the simplest and the most elegant of all games. It says something about his character — although quite what not even he knows — that his best innings came when, for one reason or another, he did not actually want to play. He cites his century and 97 against Hall and Watson on a lightning fast pitch at Kingston on MCC's 1959-60 tour; his hundred in his hundredth Test against Australia in 1968; and, in almost his last first-class innings, another hundred against them, this time for his beloved Kent. For all his complexities he was a popular person with the general public and was always prepared to find time to talk with them. As a technician, he was the nonpareil.

Batting for Kent against Essex in 1967 after it was announced that he was to lead the team to tour the West Indies later that year.

M. C. COWDREY KENT
BORN 24.12.32, PUTUMALA, INDIA

BATTING

	Matches	Innings	Not out	Runs	High score	Avg	100
Test	114	188	15	7,624	182	44.06	22
First class	692	1,130	134	42,719	307	42.89	107

BOWLING AND FIELDING

	Runs	Wickets	Avg	5 W/I	10 W/M	BB	Ct	St
Test	104	0	0	0	0	0	120	0
First class	3,329	65	51.21	0	0	4/22	638	0

TED DEXTER

John Woodcock

As a striker of the ball, at both cricket and golf, Ted Dexter possessed a wonderful talent. Whether it would have enabled him to become a great golfer we shall never know; but to say that it made him the most imposing figure at the batting crease of any Englishman since Walter Hammond is no exaggeration. If colleagues were sometimes puzzled by his train of thought, with a bat in his hand he left no-one in any doubt as to his intentions. Although an inveterate theorist, he had a method that was classically simple. He stood in the natural way, just as he would have done when he first picked up a bat, and he kept his head still. And when his courage came to be put to the test, against the West Indian fast bowlers, he gave not an inch of ground.

At school Dexter was already mature beyond his years. "How interesting that you have your boys back after their National Service," said a visiting headmaster to the Warden of Radley during a rugger match one day. Dexter had just stormed Radley into the lead. At Cambridge he was soon drawing the crowds to Fenner's — from the ladies' colleges as well as the men's (the sexes were segregated in those days). Cyril Washbrook went back to Old Trafford, after Dexter had scored 185 (105 of them before lunch on the first day) for the University against Lancashire, saying that never before had he had to field such stinging drives at cover point as from some aloof young undergraduate they were calling 'Lord Edward'.

Until railway sleepers began to be used as bats, the ball can never have been hit any harder than by Dexter. He was six feet tall and very strong with a natural sense of timing, and a full swing. I can see him now, driving an off break from Tom Veivers for six on the Melbourne Cricket Ground, the ball only just clearing the sightscreen yet still on its way up as it did so. It really was going like a rocket.

This was on Dexter's second tour of Australia — in 1962-63 when he was captain. His first, under Peter May four years earlier, had been a disappointment, though that was not entirely his own fault. Had the selectors delayed choosing May's side until after the Fourth Test Match against New Zealand in July 1958, Dexter would probably have been in the original party. Instead they picked it on the Sunday, and on the Monday Dexter, having been

c r i c k e t   h e r o e s

TED DEXTER

left out, made 52 in his first innings for England. When, eventually, he was flown out as a replacement, he remained somewhat isolated.

Communication was no more May's forte than Dexter's, and things were already going badly on the field by the time Dexter arrived. Besides Alan Davidson's late and unpredictable swing and Richie Benaud's probing spin, England had to contend with a raging epidemic of Australian throwing. Not until the tour moved on to New Zealand was Dexter seen in his true colours. The Australians had unnerved him. In New Zealand the chance to recover his confidence was gratefully, and mercifully, accepted. I say mercifully because of the style he was to bring to the game.

His next Test hundred, the following winter, was in Barbados, at the start of his only tour of the West Indies. Although he was still only 24 the West Indian fast bowlers brought the best out in him, as they did in England four years later when his 70 in 73 balls in the Lord's Test, after England had been 20 for two in their first innings, constituted the perfect response to a crisis.

Playing with the disdain for bowlers which his batting conveyed was not always to his advantage. Twenty-seven times in Tests he passed 50 without going on to get a hundred, which could be said to have been rather careless of him. When he did put his mind to it he could filibuster with the best of them. Against Pakistan at Karachi, for example, in 1961-62 he was eight and a half hours making 205, while at Old Trafford in 1964, when Australia had left England with only a draw to play for, he batted eight hours for 174.

Dexter had four full series as England's captain, taking MCC on a combined tour of India and Pakistan in 1961-62 and to Australia in 1962-63, and leading England at home against West Indies in 1963 and Australia in 1964. The chances are that he would have had charge in South Africa too, in 1964-65, had he not been unavailable for the start of that tour through contesting the constituency of Cardiff South-East in the General Election of 1964. His opponent in a straight fight, Jim Callaghan, was on his way to becoming Prime Minister, and although Dexter was a distant outsider at Cardiff he could hardly have been appointed captain of a cricket side that left for Rhodesia on polling day. In the event, the score was Callaghan, Leonard James (Labour) 30,129; Dexter, Edward Ralph (Conservative) 22,288, and in South Africa Dexter played under M. J. K. Smith.

TED DEXTER

cricket heroes

TED DEXTER

Of Dexter's 31 Tests as captain, ten were won, seven lost and fourteen drawn. Of the victories, five were against Pakistan, in the days when they travelled badly, and three against New Zealand. In that he found it hard to tune in to the ordinary mortal, or for that matter to stay in regular contact with events on the field, he fitted into no conventional category as a captain. Such, though, was his flair for the game — with the ball as well as the bat — and his indifference to criticism, that solecisms tended to be passed over. With the 16th Duke of Norfolk as Dexter's manager, MCC were represented in Australia in 1962-63 by a uniquely seigneurial pair.

Dexter's retirement in 1965, when he was only just 30, seemed sadly premature, as he had so much left to give. No doubt the independent streak that he had in him, as well as a certain restlessness, had something to do with it, and, although the distinction between amateur and professional had ended, cricket had yet to provide the sort of living he could make elsewhere. A broken leg, suffered when he was pushing his car to safety after running out of petrol, was another factor. Persuaded to reappear for a few matches for Sussex in 1968 (he had captained them from 1960 to 1965), Dexter began with an innings of 203 not out at Hastings on July 20th and was back in the England side against Australia a week later.

Dexter came out of retirement to play for the Duke of Norfolk's XI against Australia at Arundel in 1972

For 50 years I have watched the great cricketers of the world in action, and for sheer ability Ted Dexter has to rank very high among them. After Hampshire had won their first county championship in 1961 I asked Roy Marshall, perhaps the best white West Indian batsman there has ever been, how many *unplayable* balls had dismissed him that season. "Only one," he said, "and that was from Dexter at Portsmouth." When Gary Player had a round of golf with Dexter at Adelaide in 1962 he could scarcely believe his eyes, so splendid was Dexter's striking of the ball. If Severiano Ballesteros had been a cricketer, I think he would have played the game much as Dexter did — by impulse one moment and instinct the next, sometimes with circumspection and regularly with the sort of dash that is not easily forgotten.

With it all, Dexter has been thorough-going. He could not otherwise have become, in quite a short time, skilled enough as a pilot to fly himself, his wife and their two children from England to Australia in a six-seater Piper Aztec, to report, for the *Sunday Mirror*, the MCC tour of 1970-71. There is, I am sure,

c r i c k e t   h e r o e s

TED DEXTER

something of the pioneer in him, as well as of the puritan and the politician; he is both perfectionist and punter.

In his time he has mounted the pulpit to preach the gospel, bred greyhounds to win good races, devoured the *Sporting Life*, defied convention, seldom countenanced compromise, starred at athletics, excelled at rackets, owned the grandest of cars and the mightiest of motor bikes, holed the Old Course at Sunningdale in 63 strokes (the first nine holes in 29), hit the ball out of the Adelaide Oval, been as cavalier as a young man as, in due time, he grew to be congenial, and admitted to no mistakes after a disastrous first season as Chairman of the England Cricket Committee. As a batsman, even the Australians came to hold him in awe; that can be said of very few, and it is a measure of his game.

E. R. DEXTER   SUSSEX
BORN 15.5.35, MILAN, ITALY

BATTING

	Matches	Innings	Not out	Runs	High score	Avg	100
Test	62	102	8	4,502	205	47.89	9
First class	327	567	48	21,150	205	40.75	51

BOWLING AND FIELDING

	Runs	Wickets	Avg	5 W/I	10 W/M	BB	Ct	St
Test	2,306	66	34.93	0	0	4/10	29	0
First class	12,539	419	29.92	9	2	7/24	234	0

c r i c k e t   h e r o e s

BASIL d'OLIVEIRA

Robin Marlar

Single-handedly Basil d'Oliveira killed off the notion that politics and sport could be kept apart. Whether they should be regarded as separate and inviolate compartments in life's locker is another matter. To many, the plea that sport be left alone was always simplistic, and therefore an appropriate plank on which stupid sportsmen, with their brains in their feet, could base a self-centred philosophy. The recent history of international sport has shown that sport is an irresistibly easy target for politicians, whose power is all-pervading. Two wrecked Olympic Games and cricket's long struggle to hammer out a formula for its involvement with d'Oliveira's country of origin, South Africa, are obvious examples of sport's frailty when the politicians start to lean.

When John Vorster, then the grandly-titled State President of South Africa, had decided that 'Dolly', as he was already universally known, a socially classified coloured from the ironically-named Cape of Good Hope, could not be accepted in the land of his birth as a touring member of an MCC team, another principle came into play. In all sport involving international competition the visiting party must be chosen without pressure from the host country, whether that pressure be sporting or political. MCC cancelled the tour and, in cricket at least, South Africa's isolation had effectively begun.

It is a curious fact that in the final stages of cricket's resolution of the South African problem, action by politicians against the principle of unfettered selection proved the trigger for an acceptable compromise. By deploying the politicians' superior power over right of entry, the Indian Government's threat wrecked an England cricket tour, and it was the prospect of endless chaos to their international programme which persuaded cricket's leaders to devise a settlement of the South African issue which was acceptable to all the governments involved. By refusing to bend before the Indian Government's threat, preferring to cancel the tour, England's cricket held fast to the honourable tradition of rejecting direct government interference in selection which began with the d'Oliveira affair.

With the perspective of a quarter of a century we can see clearly how an extrovert, popular player came to be elevated like a totem, a rallying point for the disadvantaged and the oppressed, to such an extent that he became a

Opposite page: Basil d'Oliveira, playing for MCC, despatches a ball from Yorkshire's Brian Close at Lord's in 1968.

c r i c k e t   h e r o e s

BASIL d'OLIVEIRA

legend even before the onset of middle age. To his thousands of friends Basil d'Oliveira remained wonderfully unaffected by his status as a towering figure in sporting history as he played out his career first as a cricketer, then as a coach, and always as a good companion — albeit one a little dangerous in the small hours of the next morning.

Of course, the South African Government took all the blame and South African sport suffered all the consequences of the row. No doubt there would have been other incidents involving other sportsmen which would have sent South Africa into sporting isolation. The truth of the matter is, however, that the principal responsibility for provoking the d'Oliveira affair lay not with the South African Government or Prime Minister but with England's cricket selectors, who perpetuated yet another example of ineptitude by omitting d'Oliveira from the original selection of the team. When he was subsequently inserted as a replacement, the South African politicians naturally smelt a rat, believing, with some justification, that far from politics interfering with sport, here was an

d'Oliveira and Tom Graveney, left, on the way to the wicket to resume the batting against West Indies in the Old Trafford Test Match of 1969.

example — an intolerable example — of sport seeking to interfere with politics. The ban on Dolly was not so much an action as a reaction on the part of John Vorster.

No-one has yet completely unravelled the d'Oliveira affair. British politicians and diplomats with fine cricketing pedigrees such as Sir Alec Douglas-Home and Lord Cobham, both class county players and later presidents of the MCC, became involved. There was much discussion before and after about the acceptability of coloured, or indeed black, sportsmen in South Africa — where petty apartheid was rampant then more than now, so much so that blacks were allowed in hotels only as staff. In the end Vorster said that South Africa would not accept a team forced upon her by those with "certain political aims". Few

cricket heroes

68

BASIL d'OLIVEIRA

in England accepted the word of the selectors that they were totally unfettered by such considerations and free to choose whom they would. Amongst those who believed the selectors was the Archbishop of Canterbury!

They were, and still are, to be believed. "By their ineptitude shall they be known," is a standing jibe against England's cricket selectors. 1968 was not one of their best summers. They gathered a huge squad together at Old Trafford, including Dolly — who made 87 not out in England's second innings and took a wicket in each Australian innings — but when Ken Barrington pulled out England fielded only three front-line bowlers and were beaten. The next three Tests were drawn and Dolly appeared as a hunch selection for the last Test only because Roger Prideaux, an opening batsman, withdrew on the morning of the match. d'Oliveira made 158 in the first innings, and in the final session took the crucial wicket as Australia battled for the draw. England won and squared a series that should, on paper, have been a doddle for them.

Immediately afterwards the touring team was announced and d'Oliveira's name was not in the party. His omission was received with outrage. Tony Pawson, then cricket correspondent of *The Observer*, wrote one of his finest pieces, attacking the selectors for their lack of gratitude in not acknowledging Dolly's right to be there in the party as the man who had saved England's selectors from red faces. In the eyes of the general public, Pawson thought, they would not be forgiven. Nor were they. At that time I was doing a lot of cricket for BBC News and I remember having to telephone Billy Griffith, a dear friend, who was at that time — when there was no split between the MCC and the TCCB — the Secretary at Lord's, to ask him why this had happened and whether those concerned appreciated the enormity of what they had done. He had toured South Africa as a player and was an unhappy man, realising that there would be an outcry. Thanks to that opportunity to broadcast, my enraged reaction was one of the first. Faced by universal condemnation, the selectors then perpetuated a second chapter of folly. Tom Cartwright, a seam bowler of uniquely unusual merit, pulled out and, surprise, surprise, Basil d'Oliveira, a batting all-rounder, was then chosen as a replacement. Cartwright had been unfit when the team was originally picked! In *Wisden*, Michael Melford, as fair and rational a commentator as cricket has ever known, recorded the statement

BASIL d'OLIVEIRA

d'Oliveira on his way to 50 not out in the second innings of the 1972 Trent Bridge Test against Australia.

by Doug Insole, then chairman of the selectors, that the balance of the side had to be reviewed following Cartwright's withdrawal, and hence the selection of d'Oliveira, who had only been regarded as a batsman. No rational defence could, however, assuage public opinion either in England or South Africa. The look of the thing was wrong and everyone knew it, saw it, and understood, bar the selectors.

Theories cannot be tested *post facto* but it remains my conviction that d'Oliveira would have been admitted into South Africa had he been selected, as he should have been, at the outset. Had he been ignored thereafter, as he also should have been, at least that tour would have gone into the record books.

At that time d'Oliveira was 34. Two years earlier he had been nominated as one of *Wisden*'s five Cricketers of the Year, the cricketers' special accolade. So this cricketing dispute was not about an inconsequential player. True, 1968 was a patchy summer for him, but the talent was obvious and he was to feature in England teams for another three years.

Because of his prowess at cricket, d'Oliveira's progress was rags to relative riches on an international scale. He was playing in the league organised by the South African Cricket Board and breaking all records. Not that you could find him mentioned at that time in the pages of *Wisden*. This was a league restricted to Cape coloureds who could watch cricket at the beautiful Newlands ground but not play there.

Hassan Howa, the campaigning secretary of the SACB, used to say that there were plenty more members of his flock as good as Dolly. Others were certain that he was the best and tried their utmost to get him to England as a teenager. They failed. He was working as a printing machine operator in Cape Town when he finally secured a contract with the Middleton club in Lancashire. John Arlott, the great commentator, promoted his application. Once there he began to score heavily and take wickets so often that he was chosen for a Commonwealth side. Tom Graveney talked his team-mate into a career in county cricket and Worcestershire eventually got the d'Oliveira signature ahead of Lancashire and Gloucestershire.

As a batsman he was, above all, correct. Most players brought up on bad wickets have to understand technique. His particular strength was in his

BASIL d'OLIVEIRA

forearms and as a straight six-hitter with minimum apparent effort. That memory of Dolly remains vivid to this day. He was, on most days, a fine fielder anywhere and was important at that time as a slip catcher. His bowling action was rather special. As a natural medium pacer he was one of the rare breed of bowlers who, in their final stride, bring one foot — in his case the right — up alongside the other before delivery takes place. In coaching such rarities are known as "clickers". He had variation of pace and a natural ability to move the ball in from the offside.

These manifold cricketing gifts, this all-round competence, have furnished Basil d'Oliveira with both the knowledge and the confidence to become a fine teacher of the game. Worcestershire's many successes during the 1980s have been largely due to the capability of locally-matured players to give the team a form of inner strength to support the deeds of the county's star players. Even the great Graeme Hick has had cause to be grateful for Dolly's ability to identify bad habits and thus encourage a return to basic technique.

Who knows what the spring of that inner strength may be? Could it be an outflow from a whole lake of experience which only Dolly can know and which even he cannot communicate — even if he wished to? The escape from coloured status, recognition in another land and the huge weight of public exposure as the central figure in an international scandal are experiences given to few. Dolly has survived with his pride and integrity intact, and he remains a good mate to millions. His is quite a story.

B. L. d'OLIVEIRA WORCESTERSHIRE
BORN 4.10.31, CAPE TOWN, SOUTH AFRICA

BATTING

	Matches	Innings	Not out	Runs	High score	Avg	100
Test	44	70	8	2,484	158	40.06	5
First class	362	566	88	18,919	227	39.57	43

BOWLING AND FIELDING

	Runs	Wickets	Avg	5 W/I	10 W/M	BB	Ct	St
Test	1,859	47	39.55	0	0	3/46	29	0
First class	15,021	548	27.41	17	2	6/29	211	0

cricket heroes

BILL EDRICH

Jack Bailey

W. J. (Bill) Edrich was the most famous member of a family which could and did put a formidable team of Edriches into the field — five of them, including Bill, having played first-class cricket with distinction. Cricket was in the blood, then, and it was at a comparatively young age that Edrich left his birth-place of Norfolk for London, Lord's and Middlesex, where lasting fame lurked just around the corner. A period of qualification was followed by the award of his County Cap in 1937, at the age of 21; and in the following year he came to the notice of the world — storming to 1,000 runs before the end of May, making well over 2,000 runs in all.

Paradoxically, it was in the year of 1938 that a myth grew on the back of a string of low scores in Test Matches. Edrich lacked, they said, the big match temperament. The selectors persisted in selecting him, his detractors got redder in the face and knocked him more loudly. Edrich himself must have wondered. In all cricket that season he made 2,378 runs including six centuries; but in six Test innings he totalled 67 with a highest score of 28. That winter, the selectors, sticking to their guns, picked him to tour South Africa. Five test matches yielded only 21 runs. His detractors had a field day.

It was in the final innings of that series that Edrich dispelled, once and for all, any question of not being suited to the big occasion. That final test match at Durban saw him follow the expected low score in the first innings with a magnificent 219 in the second. It was a timeless test in which England made 654 for 5 in the final innings, 41 runs short of victory, the match being drawn because after ten days of endeavour, interrupted by rain, there was a boat to catch for England.

Nobody can have enjoyed the long journey home more than Bill Edrich, now thoroughly vindicated, an albatross lifted from around his neck. After a distinguished war, in which he flew in Bomber Command and was awarded the DFC, he began anew where he had left off. In 1946/7 his great qualities came to the fore in Test matches in Australia. Then, in 1947, he and Compton took on and put to the sword the South Africans and anyone else who cared to bowl at them. Although Compton was just ahead, Edrich also broke the record for an aggregate of runs scored in an English season, with 3,539.

Bill Edrich en route to Australia for the Test series of 1946-47.

c r i c k e t   h e r o e s

BILL EDRICH

Although destined always to be slightly overlapped by the shadow cast by his dashing partner in so many breathtaking partnerships for Middlesex and England, and although in his hands the bat became the bludgeon when compared with Compton's rapier, the many talents of Edrich were never again in question.

Celebrations at the Oval in 1953 — Edrich and Compton make their way to the pavilion following England's victory over the Australians.

His greatest strengths were spawned by his unlimited courage. It was an inner strength which bordered on stubbornness, an absolute refusal to give in. Personal defeat meant going down with all flags flying and sooner or later coming up for more. Allied to this determination, he shared with Compton an ability to communicate a love of life and a zest for the game at whatever level he chose to play. As a bowler, when bowling fast as he did in the earlier stages of his career, he 'exploded' at the bowling crease, hurtling the ball down from his small frame and short run, sometimes at a frightening speed.

Nowhere was his courage shown to greater advantage than when he himself was facing fast bowling. A fearless hooker, he was once struck on a gloomy evening at Lord's by the young Tyson. The ball hit him on the jaw and broke it. Following overnight treatment, Edrich was soon at the crease again the following morning. The pitch was untrustworthy, the ball prone to lift sharply. Edrich soon made it clear just how much this bothered him by withdrawing the bat and letting a couple such deliveries hit his chest with a resounding thwack.

He lacked Compton's instinctive grace when batting, but dealt the ball a tremendous thump — the pulled drive, the late cut and the hook bringing him a great many runs. His skill and pluck on bad wickets as well as good earned him popularity among cricket followers everywhere. They knew and loved a fighter when they saw one.

Edrich possessed a shrewd, tactical cricketing brain. This was not perhaps carried over to various judgements he made off the field where his thinking had

c r i c k e t   h e r o e s

BILL EDRICH

a certain refreshing unorthodoxy. For instance, not every cricketer would, as he did after the war, abandon professional status with a bumper benefit in the offing, to become an amateur, thus captaining his beloved Middlesex in the years between 1951 and 1957.

But he was a fine reader of a game. As a captain he made things happen. The timing of his declarations and the handling of his attack thereafter often persuaded opponents along the trail leading to disaster.

His wholehearted immersion in the game continued throughout his life. After his time with Middlesex as a player came to an end he returned to play for Norfolk, serving them with distinction with his batting and his slow off-spinners and impressing all who played under him with his leadership. He was 55 years old when he stopped playing for the county of his birth, but he continued serving Middlesex as a committee member for much longer.

An incurable romantic, like Denis Compton his great friend and colleague, he should have lived to see the day when MCC, in an eminently suitable gesture, decided to name the new Nursery Stands in honour of them both.

Another classic off-drive, another four runs for Edrich against Australia at Leeds in 1948.

W. J. EDRICH MIDDLESEX
BORN 26.3.16, LINGWOOD, NORFOLK

BATTING

	Matches	Innings	Not out	Runs	High score	Avg	100
Test	39	63	2	2,440	219	40.00	6
First class	571	964	92	36,965	267*	42.39	86

BOWLING AND FIELDING

	Runs	Wickets	Avg	5 W/I	10 W/M	BB	Ct	St
Test	1,693	41	41.29	0	0	4/68	39	0
First class	15,956	479	33.31	11	3	7/48	529	1

c r i c k e t   h e r o e s

GODFREY EVANS

John Woodcock

I don't believe it is humanly possible to keep wicket any better than Godfrey Evans used to do for England in Australia. In 1950-51 he was, so far as the eye could tell, faultless from start to finish of the Test series. He had speed, confidence, technique and timing. Yes, timing — for that is as much a part of the wicket-keeper's craft as of the batsman's or the bowler's.

There may have been others as good as Evans. From 1920 until 1950, for example, Australia had first Bert Oldfield and then Don Tallon — two superb performers. For South Africa 'Jock' Cameron and John Waite were very highly skilled, and in England, since the last war alone, Arthur McIntyre (although Evans kept him out of the England side), Billy Griffith, Keith Andrew, Alan Knott, Bob Taylor, John Murray, Bruce French and now Jack Russell, to name only some, have had wonderfully good hands.

But for sustained brilliance Evans in Australia is, for me, *primus inter pares*. Some of his leg-side work, standing up to Alec Bedser or coping with Doug Wright's more wayward googlies or diving for a thick edge off Tyson, was little short of miraculous. For some, Evans's style may have been too conspicuous. In this way he differed from the others I have mentioned. But by his methods a wicket-keeper conveys his personality, and there never was a more irrepressible cricketer than Thomas Godfrey Evans, born at Finchley on August 18th, 1920. Even in the darkest hour he would be heard to say: "We'll be there at the finish." He had the strength of an ox and a constitution that was positively awesome. However late the party of the night before, he would appear next morning like a new pin.

In his late teens, when he was knocking his opponents senseless, he had had to choose between becoming a professional boxer or a Kent cricketer. Then came the war. By the time he played the first of his 91 Test Matches he was 26. He established himself in the England side on the first of his four tours of Australia, in 1946-47, and, except twice in South Africa in 1948-49, when Griffith showed such sparkling form as to be preferred to him, he was an automatic choice until 1959.

There was nothing that Evans's Test captains were more concerned about than having to take the field without him. When sunstroke kept him out of the

c r i c k e t   h e r o e s

GODFREY EVANS

First Test in Australia in 1954-55, England lost by an innings and 154 runs. Poor Andrew, his very able understudy, found himself blamed for missing chances that never were, simply because it was said that if Evans had been there they would have been. It was, in reality, Godfrey's ubiquitousness that England had missed, as was seen when they won the next three Test Matches.

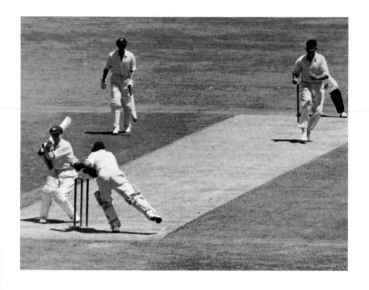

Not quite quick enough to claim a stumping this time but his first class career total came to 250.

He made bowlers bowl better and fielders field better, and there was no such thing as an Australian who frightened him.

It is a mark of the standards which he achieved that his one decidedly bad day should be so well documented. It was in 1948, when Australia scored 404 to win the fourth Test Match at Headingley and Evans missed stumping Morris off Compton and then Bradman off Laker. In the Test Trial at Bradford in 1950, when Laker took eight wickets for two runs on a treacherous pitch, Evans was as much in his element as he was at other times, taking catches that an acrobat would have been pleased to reach. At the end of the hottest day he would still be full of going.

He was also an incurably aggressive batsman, although his name is, in fact, to be found in the record books for slow scoring. Joining Compton at Adelaide in 1946-47, with England in dire straits and survival the first priority, Evans batted for 95 minutes before scoring. The Test Match was duly saved. He scored two Test hundreds, making 98 before lunch in the second of them against India at Lord's in 1952. The other was against West Indies at Old Trafford in 1950.

On his feet he was as quick as a cat, whether going down the pitch to the spinners or turning ones into twos and threes into fours. Playing for the Players at Lord's, Evans and Brian Close once ran six without the help of an overthrow, the outfield being very slow and the ball stopping just short of the long-on boundary down by the Nursery Clock Tower. On board ship Evans's speed and marvellous catching made him pretty well unbeatable at deck tennis, while as Carmen Miranda he was usually the principal turn at the Fancy Dress Ball.

c r i c k e t   h e r o e s

GODFREY EVANS

He played his first game for Kent in 1939, as a batsman, and his last in 1967, eight years after he had officially retired. Of his 1,066 first-class victims 250 were stumped, a lower percentage than Leslie Ames, his predecessor (703 catches, 418 stumpings), but higher than Alan Knott, his successor (1,211 catches, 133 stumpings). For all but 60 years the three of them brought their own very special glitter to the grounds of Kent. With the bat Evans's best season was 1952, when he scored 1,613 runs (average 28.80).

Now, many years on, he is almost completely hidden behind a dense clump of whiskers. He is still instantly recognisable, all the same, by his brisk step and trim but thick-set figure, as he makes for the press box with the latest set of prices on the current match. If the bookmakers who use his services had operated in his own day, they would have had to offer longish odds against his allowing a bye. In 1946-47 in successive Australian innings of 659 for eight and 365 there were none.

Evans claims another victim for Kent in 1957.

T. G. EVANS KENT
BORN 18.8.20, FINCHLEY, MIDDLESEX

BATTING

	Matches	Innings	Not out	Runs	High score	Avg	100
Test	91	133	14	2,439	104	20.49	2
First class	465	753	52	14,882	144	21.22	7

BOWLING AND FIELDING

	Runs	Wickets	Avg	5 W/I	10 W/M	BB	Ct	St
Test	0	0	0	0	0	—	173	46
First class	245	2	122.50	0	0	2/50	816	250

C.B. FRY

ooooooooooooooooooooooooooooooooooooooooooooooooooooooooooooooooooooooooooooooooooooooooooooo

Alan Ross

"Fry could, alike in form and in feature, have stepped straight out of the frieze of the Parthenon." So wrote H. S. Altham, who, in the same article, remarked: "Fry was beyond all doubt the greatest all-round athlete, and one of the most gifted men, that ever played cricket for England." Photographs confirm the first statement; the second goes without saying.

Around the turn of the century Fry's athletic feats were among the wonders of the age: world record long jump holder, four years in the Repton and Oxford XIs and captain of both, a soccer international who played for Southampton in the F. A. Cup Final of 1902, captain of Sussex 1904-8 and England in 1912.

Fry averaged 50 in a career that lasted from 1894 to 1921. In 1901 he hit 13 hundreds, six in succession, his total runs for the season being 3,147. For England he averaged only 31, but, as Denzil Batchelor points out in his elegant essay on Fry, that was only one run less than Victor Trumper's average and better than those of J. T. Tyldesley, Braund, or M. A. Noble.

Fry was many things besides a notable sportsman: a classicist at Oxford second only to the great F. E. Smith, a successful author and journalist, an adviser to the Maharajah Jam Sahib of Nawanagar (Ranji) at the League of Nations in Geneva. He was, in his golden youth — when in addition to the feats listed above, he acquired fame as rugby player, sprinter and high jumper — a man of all the talents, with the world apparently at his feet. The slight mystery at the heart of Fry's life is that, despite all these gifts of scholarship and athleticism, he settled for life in a comparative backwater, for 50 years nominal head of a training ship that in fact was run by his energetic and formidable wife.

Fry's marriage was an odd affair. His wife Beatie was 36, ten years older than Fry, when they married. Beatie already had two illegitimate children by Charles Hoare, a banker, and for some years after her marriage to Fry, Beatie moved between the two of them. It was Hoare who bought the training ship Mercury, which, after his death, went to the Frys and which Beatie ruled with a rod of iron. Fry's autobiography *Life Worth Living* has many virtues, but it tells nothing of his married life, omits all reference to the appalling nervous breakdown he suffered in 1929 and which lasted five years, and fails to

c   r   i   c   k   e   t   h   e   r   o   e   s

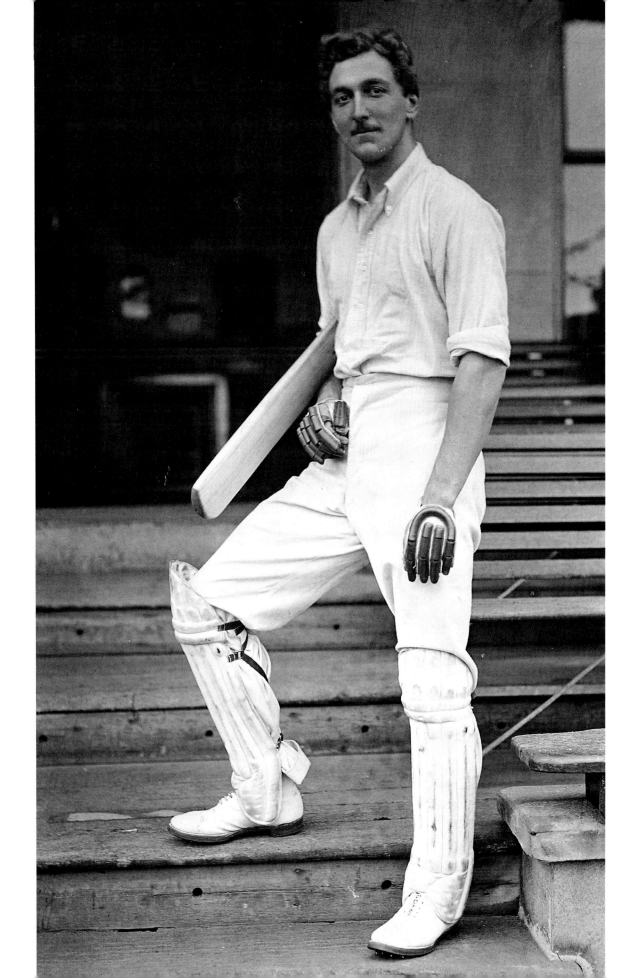

C.B.FRY

mention his numerous efforts to become a Liberal Member of Parliament. On the other hand, the book retains through several editions an account of Fry's 1934 meeting with Hitler and his undisguised admiration for the Nazi philosophy. What was it about this intellectual grandee that made him so naive about contemporary events, that despite his devotion to the classics made him so ignorant about the art and literature of his time?

There are several possibilities, the most likely being the vaunted classical education, which set him in his own mind above others and whose golden age made the present, in his eyes, of little account. For all his qualifications, Fry was so insensitive to others that he was never elected to the committee of MCC and never kept a publisher or editor for long. Reading *Life Worth Living* you get no idea of his vulnerabilities or failures, which is a pity because it would have made him seem so much more human. Instead, the book gives off an air of serenity and well-being, of comparatively small-time public success. Fry described his detailed knowledge about the workings of cars and wireless waves, his skill and devotion to dancing, but nothing about the workings of his own mind or heart.

In the nets in 1921, at the end of a long and astounding sports career.

"Cricket was a dance with a bat in your hand," Fry observed once. Yet, curiously, this Apollo, with the world at his feet, was the least dancing of cricketers. In their great partnership over the years for Sussex it was Ranji who was the natural dancer, Fry the student who had to learn the steps. And Fry did learn. He may have wished at various stages of his life to be remembered as something other than a cricketer, but it is as a cricketer more than anything else that he lays claim to our attention.

The master of back and on-side play, Fry studied the arts and techniques of batting with the same thoroughness he devoted to engines and radio. He may, to some eyes, always have seemed a manufactured player, but if so his figures point to an extraordinary mastery of his subject. Fry hit 94 hundreds, 16

C.B. FRY

double hundreds, two Test hundreds. In later life he talked the hindlegs off all and sundry, and with his monocle and chauffeur-driven Bentley, his champagne and air of effortless superiority, was not to everyone's taste. His high-handedness cost him many friends but at the wicket there was nobody to take offence.

C. B. FRY SURREY, SUSSEX AND HAMPSHIRE
BORN 25.4.1872, WEST CROYDON, SURREY

BATTING

	Matches	Innings	Not out	Runs	High score	Avg	100
Test	26	41	3	1,223	144	32.18	2
First class	394	658	43	30,886	258*	50.22	94

BOWLING AND FIELDING

	Runs	Wickets	Avg	5 W/I	10 W/M	BB	Ct	St
Test	3	0	0	0	0	—	17	0
First class	4,872	166	29.34	9	2	6/78	240	0

cricket heroes

HAROLD GIMBLETT

David Foot

I grew up believing Harold Gimblett was a more sublime batsman than Bradman. His maiden hundred, in 63 minutes at unpretentious Frome, was enshrined in West Country culture. I was just six when he missed the bus and hitched his way to the ground for the most romantic of all cricketing baptisms. In no time, along with most of my other friends around the villages of Somerset, I was able — without changing a word of the narrative — to recite the vagaries of Harold's journey to Frome and the subsequent sequence of strokes he made with Wellard's borrowed bat.

In the years that followed I took the single-track train to Taunton on half-terms and Bank Holidays. Sometimes Gloucestershire were the visitors. I don't remember Hammond from those days; I can recall virtually every cover drive from Gimblett. Indeed I made a point of sitting on the grass where I knew, at least once, I should be able to push aside my sandwich box and field the ball.

We all went just to see him. That wasn't to belittle the pace of Andrews and Wellard in tandem, the delicate efficiency of Luckes behind the stumps, the comfortable waddle up to the wickets of Hazell, the quaint, stuttering run and protruding bottom of Buse. There were greater extroverts than Gimblett, more amusing fellows. But he, in that often mysterious way in which an affinity is established between a sportsman and a crowd, was our unchallenged hero.

In retrospect, it's hard to analyse exactly why. He carried a gloomy, occasionally preoccupied, expression. He didn't throw himself about in the field — though I can't remember him ever dropping a catch or being inaccurate with that powerful underarm return — and seldom betrayed even a flicker of a smile. But, just like the farmers across the road in the market, we dropped everything when Gimblett was going to the wicket. He engendered the hustle of expectancy at Taunton, Bath and Weston (or Frome) just as Viv Richards was to do forty years later.

What thrilled us about Gimblett was his contempt for batting ritual. Like Gloucestershire's Charlie Barnett — although he belonged to an alien county and lacked comparable appreciation among the Somerset schoolboys — Harold batted with instinctive relish. He considered it his right to dispatch two half volleys in the first over. His first shot was often a straight drive which hit the

Gimblett's maiden 100 was made in only 63 minutes — with a borrowed bat!

HAROLD GIMBLETT

sight-screen first bounce. Once, against Hampshire, he hooked three times to the long-leg boundary, as if arrogantly demolishing a Southampton-based theory tried out at the outset to test his supposed vulnerability.

Lord's advised him to cut out the hook shot, it is true. "Stuff them!" was his normal retort. In fact, he became needlessly paranoiac about the game's inner sanctum and the aristocrats of the Long Room. No player had more complexes. Harold had been to a minor public school in North Devon. He had social graces and a nice speaking voice. Maybe, with a kind of inverted snobbery, he felt he should have done better with his life than be a relatively poorly paid professional cricketer in a county where, according to him, half the committee didn't know anything about the game and there was too much of an ex-military presence.

Gimblett on his way to another century for Somerset, this time against Surrey at the Oval in 1951.

He bristled when he went to Lord's and was inclined to be brusque with those in authority. MCC members were to him "puffed-up buffoons in those tomato-and-egg ties." He used to tell me he was always being slighted and denied his right, as a former Test player, simply to stand in the Long Room. Privilege angered him, in any guise. He came from Conservative farming stock but his politics wavered towards the left. He worried incessantly — about what he saw as lack of money for his wife and himself in old age, about his health, about declining standards in society, about greedy landlords: a mixed bag of neuroses.

The irony is that he created so much joy. He scored 49 hundreds for his county and one for the Commonwealth XI. He played three times for England and would have gone to India but for the war. There was a later summons for the Trent Bridge Test against the West Indians in 1950. The idea was for him to take over from the injured Hutton and to get after Ramadhin and Valentine. A nation approved. He suddenly developed a carbuncle whose throbbing, untimely presence was avidly charted in all the public prints except *The Lancet*. Many of us believe it was a psychosomatic illness.

c r i c k e t   h e r o e s

HAROLD GIMBLETT

Batting came easy for Harold. He could score runs quite beautifully — and quickly. The timing was exquisite; he could bring out a cover drive to match Hammond's. For years he carried the Somerset batting on those countryman's shoulders. Alas, he lacked the mental fibre to do this. If, as we have said, batting came for the most part easily for him, life itself didn't. He had nervous breakdowns and went to hospital for treatment. Within the dressing room he would be morose and inconsolable after a bad run. In the end he just couldn't cope any longer. He left Somerset quite dramatically, but life after cricket tormented him almost as much. Severe arthritis added to his turmoil. The 'demons' caused him to hate increasingly the game he had adorned with such bravura. He moved impetuously into a mobile home in the New Forest to get right away from the Somerset supporters who just wanted to talk cricket. In March 1978, at the time of year when he still unfailingly thought of pre-season nets, he took his life. He was only 63.

It filled us all with regrets and even guilt. We'd basked in the manner of his 23,000 runs and his 300 at Eastbourne. We'd loved him in spite of his moods. We'd tolerated his regular harangues, directed sometimes unreasonably at county officials and cricket's rulers. Maybe we should have tried harder to understand. In one spell of depression, he told me: "What I needed was more friends in cricket. Like that lovely bloke who showed me with his umbrella the way to play inswing after my Test flop at Lord's. His name was Jack Hobbs and I went out and made 67 in the second innings." It was one of the few times I saw my idol smile.

H. GIMBLETT SOMERSET
BORN 19.10.14, BICKNOLLER, SOMERESET

BATTING

	Matches	Innings	Not out	Runs	High score	Avg	100
Test	3	5	1	129	67*	32.25	0
First class	368	673	37	23,007	310	36.17	50

BOWLING AND FIELDING

	Runs	Wickets	Avg	5 W/I	10 W/M	BB	Ct	St
Test	0	0	0	0	0	—	1	0
First class	2,124	41	51.80	0	0	4/10	247	0

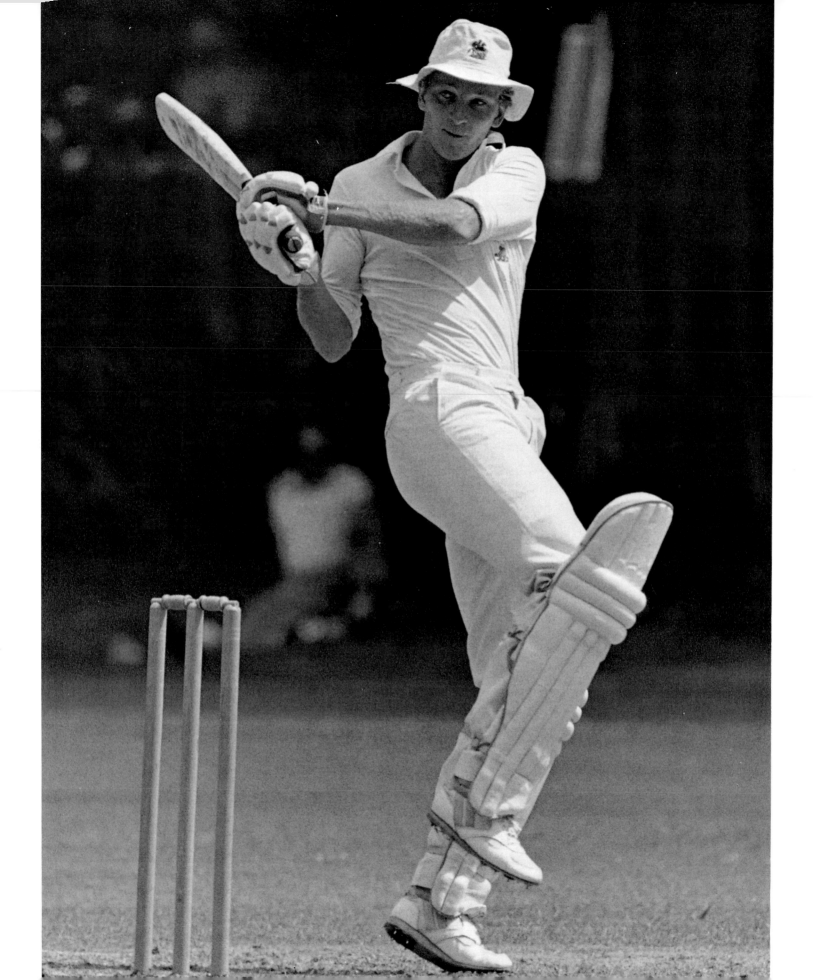

DAVID GOWER

Alan Lee

For those of us whose cricket careers have been dignified by nothing grander than the occasional painstaking 50, nudged and nicked against the rustic bowling of some remote village side, David Gower has offered pain as well as pleasure. Is it fair, we ask ourselves, that this gifted young man can find the complex art of batting so absurdly simple and can sail through the pressurised lifestyle of the modern international cricketer with no weightier concerns than the venue for his evening meal? The answer, of course, is that he cannot and does not.

Gower is every bit as misunderstood as his fellow England captain, Graham Gooch. But, while Gooch's qualities are submerged beneath a public front popularly considered solemn at best and surly at worst, Gower is widely thought to be glib, nerveless and utterly natural when, in point of fact, he is nothing of the kind.

He has, it must be admitted, committed various acts over the years which have done nothing to dispel the illusion of a modern-day cavalier. Pulling his first ball in Test cricket for four with patronising precision reinforced the myth that he finds the game all too easy; scorning a net practice to go windsurfing after his own England side had lost to an island team in the Caribbean perpetuated the notion of a casual, even careless personality. I know for a fact that he regrets the windsurfing affair; I have an idea that he would also prefer it if people did not draw quite so many conclusions from that indolent stroke at Edgbaston back in 1978. For, if there have been times when David has been amused by his public image, he has increasingly come to wish that the man in the street knew a little more of the truth.

The truth, Gower style, is the story of a man with a God-given talent to play cricket and a self-imposed commitment to the quality of life. He has never, personally, considered the two to be mutually exclusive and neither, to my knowledge, has he allowed the self-indulgences of the latter to distort the ambitions of the former. Others, however, have judged the matter more harshly and it is perhaps because of this that David Gower reached the end of the 1980s, aged 32 and ostensibly at his peak, with his future in the game clouded in uncertainty and tainted by understandable disillusionment.

David Gower deep in thought during the 1986 West Indies tour.

c r i c k e t h e r o e s

DAVID GOWER

By the end of the 1989 season he had served two spells as captain of England and, on both occasions, had lost the job in rather unhappy circumstances. He had also played more than 100 Tests and scored more than 7,000 runs for England. He could soon be the most prolific Test Match batsman ever produced by this country and yet one has the uncomfortable feeling that he is not yet about to be elevated to the ranks of cricketing legends. How can this be?

Fallibility is the clue. Great and good though I believe Gower to be there has always been a tendency, especially among us scribes, to draw attention to his niggling failings rather than his enduring virtues. So, although he might play a dozen glorious off-side strokes during an innings, we still chide him for the instinctive dart which has him caught by one of two posted gullies. Or, he might force the ball square on the legside with impeccable timing during a first-innings century yet fail to escape censure for being caught behind in the second through not getting enough bat on the shot

Perfect balance from Gower as he shows once again why he is regarded as one of cricket's greatest ever left-handers.

This frustrates him more than he indicates, for the simple reason that he cares about his performances, and about people's perception of them. While he is enviably capable of compartmentalising his life, even he cannot walk off the field and forget — nor would he want to.

A convivial companion — witty and intelligent — Gower is, however, some distance from being the iceberg many people imagine. He has nerves, and they are known to jangle quite severely on the big occasion. He also has a temper, and those who have played under him both for Leicestershire and England will testify to the short fuse which can blow if he feels he is having to suffer fools. Somehow, the warts are endearing, the awareness of mortal weaknesses comforting. They mean that Gower can and must be judged in the same way as everyone else, not as some superior being whose every slip must be microscopically examined. Look at him this way and his right to a place among the game's legends is indisputable.

He kicked off his county career with Leicestershire at the age of 18. His apprenticeship was served under Ray Illingworth, who, although sometimes exasperated by the less serious side of the Gower nature, recognised a rare talent and did as much as anyone to nurture it. Jack Birkenshaw, another early team-mate and another Yorkshireman, joins Illingworth among those whose

DAVID GOWER

advice Gower respected. They helped make him an England player by the age of 21, not just in name but in maturity. He could handle Test cricket in a fashion few so young could hope to do. It was inevitable he would go on to captain England and almost as inevitable that the affair would end in tears. Gower never could see eye to eye with Peter May, then chairman of selectors, and although he won two series as captain, his sacking was messy. Three years on, he was reappointed by Ted Dexter amid a fanfare for a new and exciting age. Sadly, England lost 4 - 0 to Australia, the partnership was terminated and Gower was then dropped.

Whatever may lie in the future for the one whose golden curls have now turned a distinguished grey, the past is full of memories. He has played some of the most vividly exciting innings I have ever seen but, out of cast character, also some of the bravest under duress. I think of his match-saving 154 not out against the West Indian pace battery at Kingston in 1981 and, more recently, of his 106 at Lord's in 1989 on the day when his credentials for captaincy were first being queried.

Gower is a man of diverse tastes, a man cricket cannot hope to own for too long. But for as long as he is around we should enjoy him, for he is a sportsman of unusual flair, style and dignity. We could do with more of his sort.

The Oval 1985 and Gower holds aloft the Ashes as England win the six-match series against the Australians.

D. I. GOWER LEICESTERSHIRE
BORN 1.4.57, TUNBRIDGE WELLS, KENT

BATTING

	Matches	Innings	Not out	Runs	High score	Avg	100
Test	106	183	13	7,383	215	43.42	15
First class	358	576	51	20,991	228	39.98	43

BOWLING AND FIELDING

	Runs	Wickets	Avg	5 W/I	10 W/M	BB	Ct	St
Test	20	1	20.00	0	0	1/1	72	0
First class	223	4	55.75	0	0	3/47	222	0

c r i c k e t   h e r o e s

W. G. GRACE

E. W. Swanton

It could reasonably be argued that more words have been written about the subject of this sketch than about any Englishman of his time and beyond. It is obviously so of any sportsman. A Bibliography of Cricket lists forty books written about him, or by him — in the latter case the work having been done by another, although in close collaboration. Of this we have evidence in the MCC library in the shape of *Cricket* published under his name in 1891 and written in its entirety in his own firm, legible hand.

In other words there is nothing new to reveal about this phenomenal man who in the time-honoured phrase found cricket a country pastime and left it a national institution. Indeed W. G. Grace, the best-known man in England — coupled according to taste with the Prince of Wales or Mr Gladstone — was himself a national institution, the country doctor, the departure of whose train from Padddington to Bristol, with silk-hatted station-master in attendance, used to await his pleasure. Three-quarters of a century on there can scarcely be a soul alive with any conscious memory of him; yet what initials today are remotely as identifiable with a man as W. G.?

This uniquely powerful public exposure from youth up was partly an accident of time. W. G. was born in 1848, and he burst on to the cricket scene at a time when this game which had been played for centuries by the villagers of the home counties had now also become the diversion of the nobility and gentry. The coming of the railways was exporting it country-wide as well as bringing its devotees to Lord's Ground at St. John's Wood and to Surrey's Kennington Oval. The growth of cricket at the public schools brought about a proliferation of clubs, both resident and wandering. County rivalries were taking shape. Into this scene came the comely son of a Gloucestershire doctor who emerged from the parental orchard and the keen tutelage therein of father, uncle, cousin and — not least — mother, to make, a little before his 16th birthday, a precocious 50 at Lord's against MCC. A year later, in 1865, he played the first two of his 85 matches for the Gentlemen, at the Oval and Lord's.

Precocity is really too mild a word to describe his youthful rise to fame. At the age of 18 he played two innings at the Oval which, Sydney Pardon wrote,

NO. 27.—DR. W. G. GRACE, F.O.S.

c   r   i   c   k   e   t   h   e   r   o   e   s

W. G. GRACE

established him "beyond all question the best batsman in England." He followed 224 for England against Surrey with 173 for Gentlemen v Players of the South, both innings not out. He earned this immediate recognition by the ascendancy he at once asserted against the hitherto predominant professional fast bowling. H. S. Altham tells us that prior to W. G. the Gentlemen had lost to the Players 19 times running. Of the next 39 games they won 27 and lost four. He had scored 10 hundreds against the Players by 1875 — evidence in abundance not only of the keenest of eyes but of dauntless pluck, for of the Lord's pitches it was said that they resembled billiards tables only in the pockets!

Grace the veteran: the beard whiter but the gaze as penetrating as it ever was.

I am attempting to remark no more than a few salient peaks in the record of a monumental prodigy. My point here is that W. G. was firmly on his pedestal several years before county cricket was more than a haphazard affair and a full decade before the dawn of Test Matches. When the Australians first tried conclusions with the mother country on its home pitches England had a ready made Champion who, at the Oval in 1880, naturally took the opportunity of scoring the first 100 against them and taking the leading part in their defeat.

Two summers in the 1870s merit special mention. In 1871, aged 23, he made his highest aggregate in a season, 2,739, with his highest ever average, 78.9. Consider that the next man, Richard Daft, could boast only 37. Bernard Darwin relates how W. G. especially relished making runs to help along a friend's benefit, and how in H. H. Stephenson's match at the Oval he was given out to the very first ball, lbw to J. C. Shaw. W. G. thought the decision a right one — so it must have been! — but paid particular attention to Shaw in his second innings of 260! Darwin supposes this may well have been the occasion when the suffering bowler summed up the matter, saying, "I puts 'em where I like, and he puts 'em where he likes." I am more inclined to attribute this remark to the much greater of the Nottingham Shaws, Alfred by name.

The most prolific week of his life was in August, 1876. He saved the match for MCC against Kent at Canterbury, making 344. After a hot, slow cross-country journey on the Sunday he took 177 off Notts at Clifton on the Monday. Yorkshire followed Notts and W. G. batted throughout Gloucestershire's innings for 318 not out — 839 in seven days, including two of them in the field while Notts were being beaten.

c r i c k e t   h e r o e s

W. G. GRACE

A specially-posed action shot of the great man at the peak of his powers.

W . G . GRACE

W. G. took time off from his doctoring to tour three times, first to Canada and the United States in 1872, followed by Australia in 1873. As an orator he kept it short and sweet, and it was in Canada that he hit upon an uncomplicated formula: "Gentlemen, I beg to thank you for the honour you have done me. I never saw better bowling than I have today, and I hope to see as good wherever I go." By substituting for bowling the words "wickets" or "prettier ladies" or "oysters" honour was satisfied all round. In later life when about to he called upon he would say: "I think I must give them one of my Canadian speeches."

The first Australian tour in 1873 was a missionary affair, all the matches being against odds. When Lord Sheffield tempted him to return in 1891 it was a very different story. W. G. was 43 and on the heavy side. It was an onerous assignment. However a fee of £3,000, plus the offer of generous expenses including the passage of his wife and two children and the provision of a locum to carry on the practice, decided the matter. (His amateurism was always more of a convention than a case of strict arithmetic.) There was some wrangling apparently, and Australia won their first rubber for ten years, 2 - 1. This however was rated a good thing since the colonials, after a proud beginning, had begun to lose heart and the enterprise was considered a success.

For some years W. G.'s batting had been looking merely mortal compared with earlier days but suddenly in 1895 came the Indian Summer which set sentimental bells ringing all over England. History tells how he began practice in the bleak March winds and continued through April. His season did not begin until May 8th and his scoring was not remarkable until on the 18th when, for the only recorded time in his life, he became flustered in making the last few runs to his 100th hundred. Fortified by some champagne at this hitherto unimaginable feat he went on to 288. When Gloucestershire faced Middlesex at Lord's two May days remained and 153 were needed for his 1,000 runs in May — a feat also never previously imagined. They duly came, and thereafter one hundred followed another — nine in all, 2,346 runs, average 51. He was 47 'and weighed untold stone.' At the end of the season four separate funds were set up which amounted to £9,073 8s 3d.

All had to be anti-climax after that, but he was coming up to 51 when he led England for the last time against Australia, and on his 58th birthday in his last

W. G. GRACE

innings for the Gentlemen, at the Oval, he made 74 before throwing his bat on the table and saying: "I shan't play any more."

The Great War with its appalling slaughter of the young all but broke the Old Man's heart. In his garden at Nottingham in the autumn of 1915 he had a stroke from which he never recovered, and on October 23, "the most wonderful chapter in the whole history of sport was closed." So wrote Altham, who may fittingly have the last word:

"Finally it may be said of W. G. that he did more to popularise cricket than any man who ever lived: his genial personality, his Jovian form, his inexhaustible vitality and stamina and enthusiasm, all combined with his prodigious prowess to make him the focus for an empire's devotion to the game."

W. G. Grace, a cricketing colossus.

W. G. GRACE GLOUCESTERSHIRE
BORN 18.7.1848, DOWNEND, BRISTOL, GLOUCESTERSHIRE

BATTING

	Matches	Innings	Not out	Runs	High score	Avg	100
Test	22	36	2	1,098	170	32.29	2
First class	879	1,493	105	54,896	344	39.55	126

BOWLING AND FIELDING

	Runs	Wickets	Avg	5 W/I	10 W/M	BB	Ct	St
Test	236	9	26.22	0	0	2/12	39	0
First class	51,545	2,876	17.92	247	66	10/49	877	0

TOM GRAVENEY

ooooooooooooooooooooooooooooooooooooooooooooooooooooooooooooooooooooooooooooooooooooooooooooo

Michael Henderson

It would be misleading to think of Tom Graveney as a man ahead of his time, yet he was in many ways the first 'modern' player produced by the English game. A batsman of peerless grace, he nevertheless had to surmount several barriers in a 23-year career spanning the arrival of Don Bradman's last Australian side and the early days of Sunday cricket.

When one reflects on the emergence of the young men who picked up the baton of English batsmanship from Compton and Hutton — May, Cowdrey and Dexter — it is easy to be deceived by notions of a golden age. In Graveney's case, the reality is colder. For years he was widely perceived as lacking Test match temperament — between 30 and 38, he was selected for a home Test in just one year, 1962, against the then far from formidable Pakistanis. Perhaps golden ages never exist — at the time. Yet Graveney was the first post-war batsman to make a hundred hundreds and 30,000 runs, who passed 1,000 runs in 21 seasons, who, uniquely, made more than 10,000 runs for two counties, who made more runs in the fifties than anyone.

With Graveney as with few others, statistics are demeaning. "If some destructive process were to eliminate all that we know about cricket, only Graveney remaining," wrote Neville Cardus, "we could reconstruct from him, from his way of batting and from the man himself, every outline of the game, every essential character and flavour which have contributed to cricket... of how many living Test match cricketers could you say as much?"

It was a career which began unremarkably. Northumberland-born, Gloucestershire-raised, Graveney turned few heads as a schoolboy, other than as a golfer of considerable promise. On army leave in 1948 from the Middle East, where he was a physical training officer, the 21-year-old played in a few benefit matches where he caught the eye. Even so, his first steps as a county player were uncertain. It took the recruitment by England of George Emmett and Jack Crapp to nudge open the door through which the young man marched. The first of his 122 centuries came against the Combined Services at Gloucester that year. Before long his offside driving brought unsolicited comparisons with Hammond and Barnett.

By 1951 he had made the first of 79 Test appearances, scoring 175 in only

TOM GRAVENEY

his second game, in Bombay. Six years went by before his next three-figure score, a double century against West Indies at Trent Bridge. Graveney's Test career lasted 18 years but recognition of his talent was never enough to earn automatic selection. Like David Gower after him, he was seen as casual in manner and performance.

The whispers began after the Lord's Test of 1953. Having put on 168 with Hutton, Graveney was bowled by Lindwall the next morning without adding to his overnight 78. Worse still, in the eyes of Freddie Brown, the chairman of selectors, he had skipped an early morning net. The night before, Hutton had watched aghast as Graveney laughed after stroking a boundary. He was judged to lack 'purpose.' If that were ever the case — and those players who radiate a sense of undiluted pleasure in performance will always be suspect — one incident helped to "put steel in my soul," as Graveney later conceded. By the end of the 1960 season, Graveney had made 19,705 runs for Gloucestershire, and led the side for two years. Then he was dumped.

Back in action in 1962 after missing a season following his move from Gloucester to Worcester, when his former county insisted on a one-year qualification period.

It is scarcely credible how professional sport, never mind cricket, was run in those days. Footballers had not yet overthrown the maximum wage. In cricket the amateur strain persisted — to Graveney's cost. When the Gloucestershire committee appointed Tom Pugh, an Old Etonian club cricketer of limited ability, as captain for 1961 and not only that, but also replaced Graveney as senior pro with Arthur Milton, they breached the limits of Graveney's loyalty. After serving a one-year qualification period, which Gloucestershire pressed for and won, the 34-year-old Graveney began a new career at New Road, a challenge he was to meet head-on. In his first year he made 2,269 runs, with nine centuries. Things were to get still better.

Worcestershire were not the strongest of clubs. They had never won the championship but their bowling strength, when Graveney arrived, was good enough for them to entertain thoughts of winning it. Beaten by Sussex in the

TOM GRAVENEY

first Gillette Cup final, they compensated handsomely in the two years which followed. Graveney's contribution in the championship year of 1964 was 2,385 runs. The third of his five centuries, against Northamptonshire at New Road, was his 100th. In 1965, when they retained the title, he supplied 1,768 more runs.

Welcomed back into the Test fold in 1966, he made 96 at Lord's and centuries at Trent Bridge and the Oval, where his eighth wicket stand of 217 with John Murray helped England to their solitary win over West Indies. It was the start of a late international flourish highlighted by 118 in the Trinidad Test two years later. His career ended unhappily the following summer when he was banned for three Tests after taking part in a match for his own benefit at Luton on the rest day of the Old Trafford Test.

For England he made 4,882 runs with 11 centuries, yet only one against Australia who regarded his frequent absences with puzzlement. "You simply have to play the way that suits you as a person and as a batsman," was his own judgment. For E. W. Swanton, Graveney's work was of "a bloom and style that in the middle-aged and elderly recalls an earlier generation." His admirers would endorse that as good enough.

Graveney pictured towards the end of his career in 1970, here playing for Worcester v Kent at Canterbury.

T. W. GRAVENEY GLOUCESTERSHIRE AND WORCESTERSHIRE
BORN 16.6.27, RIDING MILL, NORTHUMBERLAND

BATTING

	Matches	Innings	Not out	Runs	High score	Avg	100
Test	79	123	13	4,882	258	44.38	11
First class	732	1,223	159	47,793	258	44.91	122

BOWLING AND FIELDING

	Runs	Wickets	Avg	5 W/I	10 W/M	BB	Ct	St
Test	167	1	167.00	0	0	1/34	80	0
First class	3,037	80	37.96	1	0	5/28	550	1

WALTER HAMMOND

David Foot

Neville Cardus remarked that Walter Hammond's place in the National Gallery of Cricketers ought to be recorded by a sculpture rather than a painting. The famous photograph of him off-driving certainly suggests formidable power, the legs firmly rooted to the earth, the arms at the limit of their follow-through. There was, though, something about Hammond almost too mobile for sculpture, his light-footedness denying the apparent heaviness of build, the thickness around the hips and across the shoulders. He was more an illustration to some law of aerodynamics, a sketch made by Leonardo to suggest propulsion or flight. Light as a dancer in movement, Hammond had the quickness of eye and reflex that made him one of the world's great devourers of slip catches.

Hammond's Test career began in 1927-28 in South Africa and ended twenty years later in Australia, when, captaining England, he failed miserably. He was then 44 years old, six good seasons having been lost to the war. In 1938 against Australia in England he had averaged 67, in 1936-37 in Australia 58. His greatest triumph, though, was early in his career. In 1928-29, in Australia, aged 25, he made 905 runs at an average of 113 in a series that England won easily. By the time Australia next came to England, Bradman was in full flow and for the next two series Bradman easily outscored him.

For Robertson-Glasgow, though, statistics, which might have relevance in Bradman's case, had none in Hammond's. "To me," he wrote, "he is, quite simply, the greatest cricketer who began in the last twenty years and that, too, by a long distance... In the combined arts (batting, bowling, fielding) there is not one, not Bradman, not Constantine, who could stand a full and unbiased comparison with Hammond as he showed himself in the decade from 1925 to 1935; when he would make a hundred or two against Australia, then bowl down their first three wickets, then make with ease a slip-catch which others would not merely miss but would not even have rated as a miss." It was Hammond's presence to which Robertson-Glasgow paid final tribute: "A combined power and grace that I have never seen in any other man.

In his twenties Hammond was an adventurer, a batsman whose natural correctness enabled him to go forth against all-comers. He went to meet the

Of Walter Hammond Robertson-Glasgow said: "A combined power and grace that I have never seen in any other man"

WALTER HAMMOND

Hammond in maturity; almost balletic delicacy and poise.

bowler, rarely letting the bowler come to him. As he matured he gave himself more time, scoring as heavily off the back foot as once he had off the front. He rarely hooked, it is claimed, but more because he had little need to rather than because he could not. Some great players become less attractive and successful on return to their counties or in festival cricket. Not so Hammond, who suggested reserves of pleasure as well as of mischief. He had his setbacks in health, as well as in form, so that there was never anything of the comfortably settled or predictable about him, always an element of tension and danger.

Hammond played for Gloucestershire from 1920-51, missing the season of 1926 due to illness. At county grounds he exuded affableness, his dominating stature as a cricketer moulded to a country context. Playing for five of his best years under B. H. Lyon, when Gloucestershire were twice second in the championship, he was rarely out of the game; opening the bowling often, since Gloucestershire possessed no bowlers of true pace, taking startling and nonchalant catches at slip, and then, as often as not, after Charlie Barnett had set the innings going, batting out the day, or for as long as he felt it necessary.

In 1939 Hammond captained Gloucestershire for the first time, the county coming third. His captaincy of England, in 1946-47, was less successful; not only was his own contribution negligible, but he often travelled about Australia apart from his team, generally remaining aloof. If this was a disappointing end to Hammond's career, his last pre-war appearances, captaining England in South Africa and at home against the West Indies, were more fitting to a cricketer of his gifts. In South Africa Hammond's scores were 24, 58, 181, 120, 1, 61 not out, 24, 140, and against West Indies, when England won the series 1 - 0, Hammond scored 14, 30 not out, 22, 32, 43, 138. These were not the scores of his heyday, nor were they made in quite the same manner, but they were a fairer epitaph.

Hammond died in 1965, in South Africa, his retirement years in that country not always of the happiest. Genius does not necessarily command the peace and prosperity it deserves and Hammond's fame was for some time bruised. But nothing could take away the memories of those who saw — or even read about — him in the golden years of 1927-30, or who witnessed his 240 at Lord's against Australia in 1938, when, after England were 31 for 3, they ended the day 409 for 5, Hammond 210 not out.

c r i c k e t   h e r o e s

WALTER HAMMOND

That innings, in company with his double trouncing of McDonald at Old Trafford in 1927 — 99 and 187, the latter score made in three hours, five minutes, with four sixes and twenty-four fours — is one of dozens that were unique in their impact. "There was a proconsular presence about Walter," Denzil Batchelor wrote in *The Book of Cricket*. "His torso was majestic enough to make a ship's figure-head; his face had a look of lordship about it. Nor was his dominating quality confined to his appearance. It gave a true picture of the man in action. Hammond didn't walk to the wicket. He strode."

In a curious comparison with Bradman, whom he rated the more dynamic player, Cardus wrote of Hammond that, for all his gifts, he could be kept quiet, "Bradman never." Hammond's methods, as they developed under Jardine, Cardus described as: "static, with genius transforming to greatness a conventional classicism." That was not initially the case. "I believe," Cardus continued, "that under Maclaren's captaincy, Hammond would have remained to the end a match-winning Test match batsman, an annihilator of all bowling, not only a beautiful stylist, weighted with responsibility, and glad of an escape into the gentler atmosphere of Gloucestershire cricket. For it is to the Hammond of county matches that we have had usually to look for the free and happy Hammond."

It is the penalty of great Test batsmen, in an era when they stand alone, and when so much depends upon them, that they should find some of the fun and adventure going out of the game. Hammond lost something in the process, as did Hutton in his turn.

W. R. HAMMOND GLOUCESTERSHIRE
BORN 19.6.03, DOVER, KENT

BATTING

	Matches	Innings	Not out	Runs	High score	Avg	100
Test	85	140	16	7,249	336*	58.45	22
First class	634	1,005	104	50,551	336*	56.10	167

BOWLING AND FIELDING

	Runs	Wickets	Avg	5 W/I	10 W/M	BB	Ct	St
Test	3,138	83	37.80	2	0	5/36	110	0
First class	22,389	732	30.58	22	3	9/23	819	3

c r i c k e t   h e r o e s

LORD HAWKE

Derek Hodgson

Lord Hawke is regarded today as a distant, autocratic Victorian figure who first achieved renown by pulling up a Yorkshire team of high ability and dissolute ways by their bootstraps, going on to be one of the most influential figures in cricket in the first half of this century. His words "Pray God no professional shall captain England" have been remembered as the epitome of obsolescent elitism. Read any critique that associates MCC and the amateur player with snobbery or 'old school tie' government of the game and Hawke's name is sure to be included.

There was much more to Martin Bladen Hawke. He was the seventh Baron in a line founded by Edward Hawke, an 18th century admiral whose philosophy was: "to totally destroy the enemy whenever and wherever he can be met." In his most famous victory over the French, on November 20, 1759, he attacked 20 ships of the line, in a gale, off one of the most terrifying coasts in the world — Quiberon Bay in Brittany. When the captain expostulated at the risk of taking the 100-gun flagship *Royal George* into the rocky bay — in darkness, in a howling wind — Hawke replied: "Mr Robinson, you have done your duty in pointing out the dangers, now obey my orders and lay me alongside the French admiral."

Not surprisingly the French were routed and a grateful nation, almost 20 years later, created Hawke a Baron. Almost 150 years later the sixth Baron, a Lincolnshire clergyman, fathered Martin Bladen — who would recall that his father, a much gentler strain, could recite without error the whole of Goldsmith's *The Deserted Village* and was an authority on gladioli and hollyhocks. Perhaps the martial spirit descended through the ladies, for the boy's grandmother attended the famous ball in Brussels on the eve of Waterloo and the following day rode out to Quatre Bras "to see what was going on."

It was while a schoolboy, playing cricket in his holidays, that he was invited to appear for the Yorkshire Gentlemen where his batting caught the eye of the Reverend E. S. Carter who, with the Earl of Londesborough, was one of the founders of the Scarborough Festival. Hawke had already appeared for Yorkshire in 1881 before winning a Cambridge blue the following year and adding two more in 1883-85, captaining the University in his final year and

Martin Bladen (Lord) Hawke led Yorkshire to eight championships in his 27 years as captain, during which time the county finished out of the top four on only four occasions.

LORD HAWKE

leading them to a seven wicket victory over Oxford. The intervening year was spent on military duty — he also became a captain in the Prince of Wales' Yorkshire Regiment.

Yorkshire were willing to name him captain as a 22-year-old but he was shrewd enough to wait and listen to the likes of Tom Emmett and Louis Hall. Not until 1886 did he assume complete control of the side and from that moment the rise of the White Rose was assured. In all he led the side for 27 seasons, turning what was described, on his arrival, as 'a team of alecans' into one capable of winning eight Championships (and only four times finishing out of the top four). He was never afraid to ask the advice of his senior professionals, in public — and to follow it — but once his mind was made up he acted, like his famous forefather, swiftly and decisively.

This was never more evident than in his treatment of players. He sacked two of the game's greatest left-arm spin bowlers, Ted Peate and Bobby Peel, for misconduct; three highly promising young players, all of whom were thought to be England prospects, went the same way. Another man, who had spent years on the fringe of the team and given loyal service, was despatched after he had made no effort to take a high catch on the Lord's boundary.

T. L. TAYLOR.

…WKE, (CAPTAIN)

Copyright.
PHOTO HAWKINS, BR…

Such was his fame that Hawke, left, even featured in a series of postcards.

Less publicised and less obvious were his efforts on behalf of his players, most of whom came from poor backgrounds and had little skills outside of their cricket. Under Hawke, Yorkshire led the way in promoting the welfare of their professionals, establishing regular summer and winter pay, benefits, pensions, and merit marks (bonuses awarded for exceptional performances, not just in figures but according to the conditions and the opposition). He was not a rich man but many of the merit mark payments came out of his own pocket. It was Hawke who devised Yorkshire's distinctive white rose badge, the eleven petals signifying the members of the team. Hawke's personal colours — Cambridge blue, Oxford blue, and gold — became the club's.

As a player he was a right-handed batsman of middling ability who scored 1,000 runs in 1896 and in four more summers came close to that figure. Pelham Warner said he: "could drive very hard and late cut well... more than once he pulled Yorkshire out of a tight place." He took more teams abroad than any other captain — before or since — to Australia, India, Ceylon (Sri Lanka), Canada, USA, South Africa and West Indies and played for England in five

c r i c k e t   h e r o e s

LORD HAWKE

Tests, captaining them in four — all at a time when travelling anywhere would be considered a real hardship by modern standards.

When in England he would always try to get home in order to accompany his mother to church on Sunday. Warner remembered him for passing on what Hawke considered as the "two essentials in choosing an eleven" — good temper and good manners.

He was simultaneously both President and captain of Yorkshire and was instrumental in taking the selection of England teams from the Test ground authority to MCC; he went on to become chairman of selectors and President of MCC.

As to his infamous dictum on professionals I quote from *The Official History of Yorkshire CCC*: "In 1925 when Cec Parkin, in a newspaper, attacked Gilligan's captaincy of England in Australia, Hawke told Yorkshire's AGM: 'Pray God no professional shall ever captain England. I love and admire them all but we have always had an amateur Skipper and when the day comes when we shall have no more amateurs captaining England it shall be a thousand pities.' "

It is perhaps easier to understand, if not agree with, such sentiments now than it was then. Professional captaincy has now ruled long enough for fair comparisons to be made with a system that, while growing rapidly obsolete, was not without its virtues. Hawke knew his Gentlemen and his Players; he also knew his players and his gentlemen.

M. B. (LORD) HAWKE   YORKSHIRE
BORN 16.8.1860, GAINSBOROUGH, LINCOLNSHIRE

BATTING

	Matches	Innings	Not out	Runs	High score	Avg	100
Test	5	8	1	55	30	7.85	0
First class	633	936	105	16,749	166	20.15	13

BOWLING AND FIELDING

	Runs	Wickets	Avg	5 W/I	10 W/M	BB	Ct	St
Test	0	0	0	0	0	—	3	0
First class	16	0	0	0	0	—	209	0

PATSY HENDREN

Marcus Williams

Patsy Hendren is not always quoted in the same breath as the game's immortals, but his career statistics place him very high indeed in the cricketing panoply: 170 centuries, second only to Hobbs; 57,611 runs, third only to Hobbs and Woolley; 1,000 runs or more in a season 25 times, beaten only by Grace, Woolley, Cowdrey, Mead, Boycott and Hobbs; exceeding 3,000 three times, equalled only by Sutcliffe and Hammond, and 2,000 twelve times. He was also an outstanding fielder, which first brought him to prominence, and more than 750 catches were pouched in his safe hands.

Figures alone, however, tell little of the man. The universal image of Patsy — it is hard to imagine anyone calling him by his given names, Elias Henry — is of a perky, genial character, an entertainer who loved to play cricket and was as much a favourite of the Lord's crowd in the inter-war years as Compton and Edrich were to be afterwards. The tremendous ovation he received in his final match there, against Surrey in 1937 when he fittingly made a hundred, was proof. He was popular too with his fellow players and would have the dressing-room in uproar with his mimicry and wit.

Hendren in 1930, shortly after his four double centuries and two centuries on the tour to West Indies.

Born of Irish extraction at Turnham Green, near Chiswick, in 1889, Hendren, like many, graduated to Middlesex via the Lord's ground staff. He prided himself that he was never coached and modelled his play on the Lancastrian, Johnny Tyldesley, another compact figure who excelled in the speed of his footwork. Square and muscular, Hendren crouched slightly at the wicket, which made him appear smaller than he actually was. As with all the great batsmen, he possessed a sound and orthodox defence, but his strength and ability made him a master of all the strokes except the late cut. He excelled in the hook and square drive, and late in his career developed a lofted drive to mid-wicket. Above all, he was never dull to watch.

Hendren made his debut for Middlesex (though *Wisden* and the county's history credit the appearance to his brother, Denis) in the infamous 1907 match in which A. C. MacLaren, the Lancashire captain, refused to go on beyond the second day because he claimed the pitch had been deliberately damaged by spectators. Hendren's early years in the side were not blessed with great success and though he was awarded his cap in 1909 after scoring 71

PATSY HENDREN

against a Yorkshire attack containing Hirst, Haigh and Rhodes — going down on one knee to have the cap placed on his head by his captain, Plum Warner — it was after the First World War that he really established himself as a key member of the side. He had already made his mark as a footballer, being chosen for England in a Victory international against Wales.

His performances in 1919 brought recognition as one of *Wisden*'s Five Cricketers of the Year and, after heading the national averages in Middlesex's championship-winning summer of 1920, he was selected for the winter tour of Australia. Though he was, by some distance, leading run-maker in all matches, he performed only moderately in the Tests, all of which England lost. He was to go twice more to Australia, each time enjoying greater success outside the Test matches, although on his last visit, in 1928-29, he made a superb 169 in the opening match of the rubber at Brisbane, showing great composure at a crucial stage and then unfolding a fine array of strokes to set England on the way to victory by 675 runs and a 4-1 win in the series.

Another mighty blow from Hendren, this time into the top tier of the pavilion at Lord's against Warwickshire in 1920.

Hendren enjoyed other successes overseas, not least the 1929-30 tour to the West Indies, when, passing his forty-first birthday, he revelled in the hard pitches to the extent of four unbeaten double centuries — including 205 in the second Test at Port of Spain — and two centuries, and altogether scored 1,765 runs at an average of 135.76. The achievements were all the more meritorious in that, in several of the matches, he faced Constantine bowling at his fastest with a bodyline field. The memories were not lost on Hendren, for, when he faced Constantine and Martindale at Lord's in 1933, he wore a protective cap designed by his wife. It had three peaks, the extra two covering his ears and temples, and was lined with sponge rubber.

Though Hendren's record in home Tests was inconsistent, it had its highlights. He hit successive hundreds against South Africa in 1924 and then 127 not out against Australia at Lord's in 1926, interestingly the only Test century by a Middlesex batsman on his home ground against Australia and one which gave him, a former scorecard seller, the utmost pride. When recalled to the colours against Australia eight years later he helped England to avoid the follow-on with 79 at Trent Bridge and then scored 132 at Old Trafford in the penultimate of his 51 Tests.

For almost two decades he scored prodigiously for Middlesex, frequently

PATSY HENDREN

heading the averages, run aggregates and total of centuries, and forming a famous middle-order partnership with his friend, J. W. Hearne. Hendren retired from county cricket in 1937 and went on to coach at Harrow School (his second year in charge saw the first win over Eton for 31 years), Lord's and Sussex and was Middlesex scorer from 1952 to 1960. He died in 1962. Sir Neville Cardus, writing earlier in the year, provided an appropriate epitaph: "His smile, on the field, as well as off it, is so wide that I often expected he would one day be given out 'Smile before wicket'."

E. H. HENDREN   MIDDLESEX
BORN 5.2.1889, TURNHAM GREEN, MIDDLESEX

BATTING

	Matches	Innings	Not out	Runs	High score	Avg	100
Test	51	83	9	3,525	205*	47.63	7
First class	833	1,300	166	57,611	301*	50.80	170

BOWLING AND FIELDING

	Runs	Wickets	Avg	5 W/I	10 W/M	BB	Ct	St
Test	31	1	31.00	0	0	1/27	33	0
First class	2,574	48	53.62	1	0	5/43	754	0

GEORGE HIRST

David Hopps

If county cricket is blessed with a great protector, he must surely be cast in the image of George Herbert Hirst. Lord Hawke, Yorkshire's autocrat, praised Hirst as the greatest county cricketer he knew; Sir Leonard Hutton described him as the most lovable; Bill Bowes suggested he would never meet a better coach — or better man. Yorkshiremen in the early 1900s loved to boast that the world's best all-rounder came from Kirkheaton, batted right-handed and bowled left. Whether the rightful claimant was Hirst or Wilfred Rhodes was a matter for self-indulgent debate. If Rhodes's superior Test record is persuasive, Hirst's brilliance is most apparent in his colossal contribution to county cricket's good fellowship. By the time he stood on the pavilion balcony at the 1921 Scarborough Festival to announce his retirement, 'George Herbert' was 50 years old.

Hirst did the double 14 times — only Rhodes, from the same stone-built village near Huddersfield, dug into the slopes of the Pennines, can surpass that. His double-double in 1906 (more than 2,000 runs and 200 wickets) is unparalleled in its enormity. Hirst's homely retirement speech captured the gentle spirit of a man whose smile, Lord Hawke tells us, "went right round his head and met at the back."

"If I've had any broad views on what they call the game of life, I've learned them on the cricket field," Hirst said. "What can you have better than a nice green field, with the wickets set up, and to go out and do the best for your side? I leave first-class cricket to those who have got to come. I hope they'll have the pleasure in it that I have had."

The father of inswing bowling, Hirst's 'swerve' was almost as revolutionary a force as cricket embarked upon a new century as Bosanquet's unravelling of the googly a few years later. It provided the stocky, broad-shouldered Yorkshireman with a stature well above his 5ft 6ins. He preferred to bowl into a half-headwind, as a left-arm bowler, breezing in from third man, and was particularly deadly when the ball was new or there was moisture about. To this attribute he added a slower ball, a finger-spinner, but the virtues of spin and swerve always bowed to his oft-stated imperative: "Length first." Vital advice from someone troubled by a recurring leg strain for vast portions of his career.

GEORGE HIRST

Hirst's batsmanship was not of the classical vein. It was vigorous, bold and blunt, packed with what the poet William Kerr referred to as "brave Chaucerian pulls." From an unorthodox two-eyed stance, his hearty pull shot, occasionally hauled through square leg off one knee, was as characteristic as Ranji's leg glance.

Such a wholehearted cricketer could have been forgiven a rest in the deep. But when *Wisden*, in 1901, complained of fielders resembling "little mounds of earth" Hirst was held to be an exception. Straight driving was then the fashion and mid-off was nowhere to hide. D. L. A. Jephson wrote: "You may as well drive through a brick wall as pass those iron hands."

Hirst's schooling ended when he was 10 years old. *Vanity Fair* was to remark in 1903: "If he is not a great linguist, he is at least a complete master of the West Riding dialect." He worked as a wirer for a hand-loom weaver, then at a local dye works before his first Yorkshire trial at the age of 18. Hirst recalled: "I wore a sixpenny belt with a snake-clasp and brown boots. My shirt was blue but I got a white one with my first money."

George Hirst as portrayed on a postcard at the end of the last century.

His Yorkshire debut, under Lord Hawke's all-encompassing rule, duly arrived in 1893. England's call followed six years later at Nottingham, W. G.'s farewell Test. By then his brisk, straight left-arm had gained in stealth; as a batsman, who began at No. 10, he had proved Grace's early observation that, "the fellow can bat a bit as well." Throughout his career his doughtiest displays came in the hour of greatest need. Lancashire learned to rue him. In Hirst's eyes, "When you're a batter and a bowler, you're twice as happy," and his first double, in 1896, began to quieten those sages who felt his all-round involvement would become an impossible burden.

The following season, he was involved in one of Yorkshire cricket's most comic interludes, an affair which had lasting repercussions for his own career. Bobby Peel, Yorkshire's left-arm spinner, had a fondness for the bottle. Late at night his drunkenness was a passing embarrassment, but on the morning of a match it was liable to incur Hawke's wrath. Hirst good-naturedly put Peel to bed, before informing his Lordship that he had become "a little queer in the night." His exertions proved in vain as Peel took to the field much the worse for wear. Peel never played for Yorkshire again. Rhodes replaced him and a partnership was forged which was to last beyond the First World War.

cricket heroes

GEORGE HIRST

Hirst's record in 24 Tests, 21 against Australia, was sound enough — 790 runs at an average of 22, 59 wickets at 30 apiece. A first tour under A. E. Stoddart in 1897-98 was followed with a place in Pelham Warner's party six years later, yet he did not relish the hot, sleepless nights and the unyielding pitches. Astonished to find a Melbourne 'sticky' during his second visit, Hirst's response spoke of his long-suffering. "When I was in Australia before, I only saw one wet wicket, and that was hung up to dry," he remarked.

If he possessed feelings of failure, they were banished during one remarkable week in 1902 as he was the scourge of the Australian tourists, twice dismissed for less than 40. In the first Test Australia fell in poor light for 36, of which Victor Trumper made half. Hirst's return of 11-4-15-3 was overshadowed by Rhodes's 7-17 but as sound a judge as C. B. Fry opined that there was no clearer case of a bowler taking wickets because of his partner's labours.

Rain rescued the Australians and, somewhat shaken, they journeyed to Headingley where they faced Yorkshire on a treacherous surface which today would attract howls of protest. There is reason to surmise that being Headingley the ball swung lavishly. In the second innings Hirst (7-4-9-5) and F. S. Jackson (7-1-12-5) bundled out the tourists for 23. Hirst described the ball that bowled Trumper as the best of his life.

Hirst's apocryphal grunt to Rhodes — "We'll get 'em in singles" — as England's last pair saved the follow-on against Australia at The Oval later that summer was a tale relished by at least one of Kirkheaton's finest. Rhodes regarded it as flippant. Seven years on came another Ashes confrontation. On a rain-affected Edgbaston pitch, Hirst (9-86 in the match) joined forces with Colin Blythe (11-102) to inspire England's only success.

The century had turned before Hirst gave clue to his greatness. He matured gradually, perhaps urged ahead by Rhodes's mounting reputation. His new-fangled weapon of swerve led Sammy Woods, of Somerset, to wonder: "How the devil can you play a ball that comes in at you like a hard throw-in from cover-point?" Hawke wondered in 1901 if anyone had ever swerved a ball more. Astonishing, then, that Somerset beat Yorkshire that season by 279 runs and left Hirst to brood on figures of 1-189.

Achievements piled high. Hirst's 341 against Leicestershire in 1905 remains Yorkshire's highest individual score. Spared the enthusiasm of a young

GEORGE HIRST

Hirst was variously described as: the greatest county cricketer of his era, the most lovable, the best coach and the world's best all-rounder.

GEORGE HIRST

substitute fielder, Tom Jayes, he felt he would have reached 400. But for sheer wholeheartedness, the triumph of 1906 remains unsurpassed: 2,385 runs at 45.86; 208 wickets at 6.50. He rubbed his legs with oils to prevent them seizing up; he often bowled with a bandaged knee. Asked if anyone would ever repeat the feat, he replied: "I don't know, but whoever does will be very tired." The crowning glory against Somerset at Bath (111 and 117 not out; 6-70 and 5-45) remains county cricket's greatest individual performance.

Hirst's powers diminished imperceptibly. Indeed, the advent of a Roses match proved an elixir of youth. His 9-23 against Lancashire at Leeds in 1910 was judged the feat of the season. A year later at Old Trafford he followed six wickets with 156. From the last uninterrupted season before the Great War, he salvaged his final double. In 1914 he still had time to bowl Jack Hobbs after a magnificent century at Park Avenue. Hobbs's final six, moments earlier, had knocked back the hour hand of the pavilion clock. "You should have knocked it on to six-thirty, Jack, then we'd have been rid of you," complained the unfortunate bowler, Alonso Drake.

Time *was* rushing on for Hirst but, extraordinarily, war did not force his retirement. Approaching his 48th birthday, he dominated Yorkshire's first post-war match against the MCC at Lord's with an undefeated 180. For many spectators, barely back from the Services, it was perfect therapy.

Long after his retirement, at 58, Hirst bowed once more to the charms of the Scarborough Festival. He made a single, then was bowled by Bowes. The response was typically gracious. "A grand ball that, lad," he said, "I couldn't have played that when I was good."

G. H. HIRST YORKSHIRE
BORN 7.9.1871, KIRKHEATON, YORKSHIRE

BATTING

	Matches	Innings	Not out	Runs	High score	Avg	100
Test	24	38	3	790	85	22.57	0
First class	825	1,215	151	36,323	341	34.13	60

BOWLING AND FIELDING

	Runs	Wickets	Avg	5 W/I	10 W/M	BB	Ct	St
Test	1,770	59	30.00	3	0	5/48	18	0
First class	51,282	2,739	18.72	184	40	9/23	607	0

cricket heroes

JACK HOBBS

E. W. Swanton

MR JACK HOBBS.

A 1926 illustration of England's first cricketing knight.

If to be master of one's craft and to wear one's success with modesty and humour is the beau ideal of a sportsman then Jack Hobbs filled his role to perfection. He did so, moreover, over a remarkably long span. Frank Woolley used to say that only those who had seen Jack bat before the war (the first one, of course) could bear witness to the complete, uninhibited stroke-play of those early days — and the young pair played in 19 Tests together pre-war, starting in 1909.

It was just quarter of a century later when in George Duckworth's benefit match at Old Trafford Jack made his 197th hundred. (Pat Hendren with 170 hundreds is next on the list.) A month or two later he bowed quietly out of the Surrey XI. He was coming up to his 52nd birthday, and the legs that had carried him to more runs than anyone had ever made — 61,237 of them — had begun to protest too much for his comfort.

Three men, I would suggest, each in his generation have stood unrivalled in the art of batsmanship, and it seems curiously fitting that their careers should have touched one another. W. G. Grace, who in performance and personality alike had towered over the cricket scene for the best part of forty years, took the field at the Oval for the Gentlemen of England on a chilly spring day of 1905 and saw the Surrey colt Hobbs (J. B.) open the innings and make 88 in just two hours. It was Jack's first first-class match and one of W. G.'s last. The overlapping of Hobbs and Bradman was more protracted, beginning in the 1928/9 Test series in Australia and culminating in Jack's last Test Match, at the Oval in 1930. The Don retired in 1948. Thus it could be said that the genius and influence of the immortal trio pervaded the batting art for three-quarters of a century.

Jack was born at Cambridge on December 16, 1882, son of the Jesus College groundsman and played his first cricket on that sublime stretch all but in the middle of the town known as Parker's Piece. There he came under the influence of the great Tom Hayward.

It is a matter of history that Jack first applied for a trial to the adjacent county of Essex, who simply were not interested. If they had been, who can tell how long it would have been before his inherent quality took him to the top?

c r i c k e t   h e r o e s

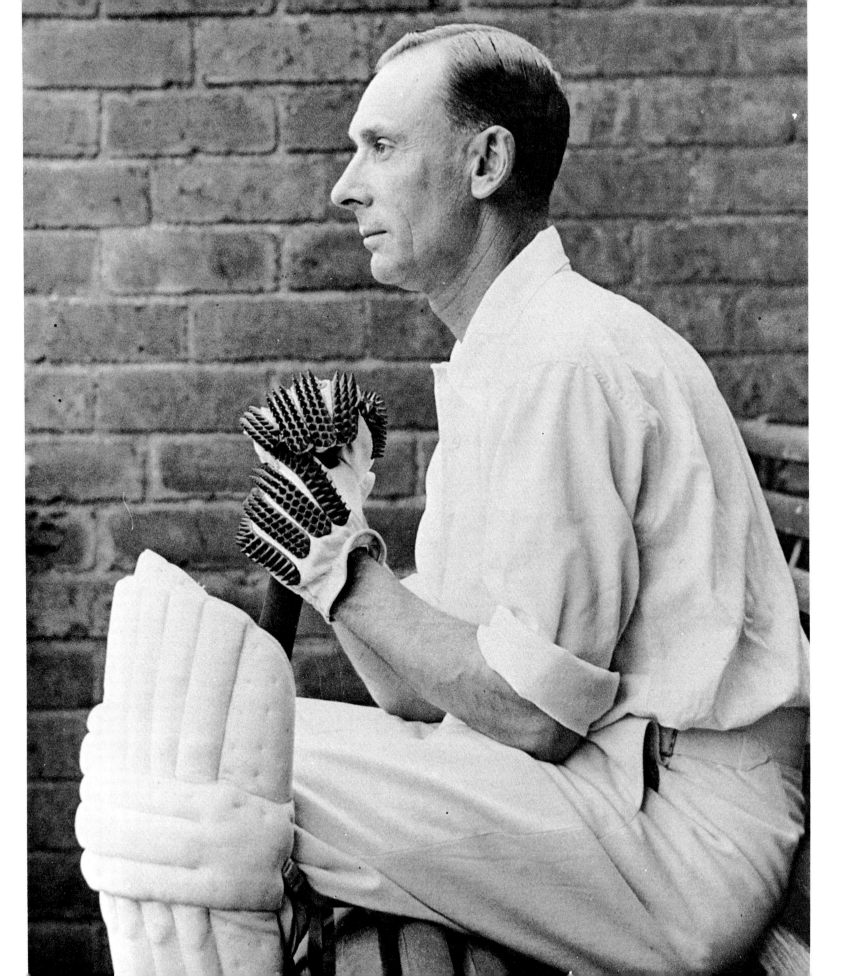

JACK HOBBS

What is sure is that Hayward's recommendation to Surrey in 1903 gave him the ideal start. Within two years he was going in first with his mentor on Sam Apted's perfect pitches. Fate saw to it that after the Gentlemen Surrey's first opponents were Essex, who had spurned him. Jack made 155, and Lord Dalmeny (soon to become the Earl of Rosebery) forthwith gave him his cap, one of the swiftest awards ever.

Fortified by such an expression of confidence, he made 1,317 in that first summer, and did even better in his second. In his third he played for the first of 49 times for the Players and was chosen for the MCC 1907/8 tour to Australia. He was already rated the third best professional batsman after Hayward and J. T. Tyldesley. Naturally Jack took advantage of the constant example at the other end of the man "on whose superb example," said *Wisden*, "his own style of batting has obviously been modelled."

Hobbs, left, and Herbert Sutcliffe: regarded as England's finest opening partnership.

Although in the more formalised cricket of Jack's earlier days the attack was generally aimed at or outside off-stump, the Surrey pair were adept at exploiting the leg-side strokes. Jack's repertoire was, however, complete and remained so when in his later years he opened his stance somewhat, the better to cope with the greater prevalence of in-swing. He was of average height and physique, his power deriving from instinctive footwork and perfect timing. He regarded balance and the positioning of the feet as the keys to batting. His advice was always: "Keep it simple."

Whether England and Surrey were doing well or ill there was an extraordinary consistency about his performance. Over his career in England he averaged 0.07 below 50; in Australia it was 51, on the South African mat 68. Yet no-one gave away his wicket more frequently when it mattered little; often enough he reckoned that 100 was sufficient. He had 15 Test hundreds, and on his fifth and last tour of Australia, as senior professional to A. P. F. Chapman, aged 47, said goodbye at Melbourne with two superb innings of 142 and 65. His overall Test average was 56. He was lucky with his opening partners, but how much luckier were those younger men, Sandham and Sutcliffe, in his presence at the other end! Hayward and he reached 100 together 40 times; with Sandham it was 66 times, with Sutcliffe 26. In all, his tally of such partnerships was an unbeatable 166.

He was a marvellous judge of a run, and despite all the thousands of singles

JACK HOBBS

that he and Sutcliffe stole together he was run out only once — from a direct throw by Bradman, following Sutcliffe's call! The number of run-outs he himself achieved was legion. He was the best cover-point of his day, moving around at times apparently uninterested until someone took a liberty. Then came the swoop, the flick and another victim saw his error too late.

Jack was a practising Christian all his life, a fact of which I was reminded not long ago by a reader who remembered how on Sunday mornings his parents used to take their family to church by a longer route from their Streatham home for the pleasure of seeing the Hobbses similarly on their way. This was the sort of veneration which Jack and other household names of his day merited and received. He enjoyed a glass of wine and a cigar, and in congenial company was excellent value. I admired him enormously, but must declare an interest. Leaving Lord's once during a Test at tea-time he explained his going to John Warr: "I've had a good day and seen all my friends, and I can read Jim Swanton in the morning." No compliment ever pleased me more.

J. B. HOBBS SURREY
BORN 16.12.1882, CAMBRIDGE

BATTING

	Matches	Innings	Not out	Runs	High score	Avg	100
Test	61	102	7	5,410	211	56.94	15
First class	825	1,315	106	61,237	316*	50.65	197

BOWLING AND FIELDING

	Runs	Wickets	Avg	5 W/I	10 W/M	BB	Ct	St
Test	165	1	165.00	0	0	1/19	17	0
First class	2,666	107	24.91	3	0	7/56	334	0

Hobbs: a master of the cricketing craft.

LEN HUTTON

Marcus Williams

If he had achieved nothing else in cricket, Len Hutton assured his immortality in the game with one innings at the Oval in 1938. That it was a monumental feat of concentration, lasting for 13 hours 20 minutes, was a matter of awe. That it produced the highest innings hitherto in Test cricket, 364, seized the attention and admiration of the nation. That he eclipsed a record previously held by Don Bradman (334 at Leeds in 1930, an innings which Hutton himself had watched as a spellbound schoolboy) added to the aura of the occasion. That Hutton was aged only 22 made him a very youthful living legend. His, career, however, was to be filled with further honours: the first regular professional captain of England, the man who won back the Ashes after a gap of nearly 20 years, the first professional elected to membership of MCC before the end of his playing days, and the second (after Hobbs) to be knighted for services to cricket.

Len Hutton at the Oval in 1938, on his way to 364, and overtaking Bradman's record of 334 set in 1930.

Born at Fulneck, a mile from Pudsey, in 1916, into a keen cricketing family, he had grown up in Yorkshire's hard cricket school. Graduating from Pudsey St Lawrence, a club which had also nurtured John Tunnicliffe and Herbert Sutcliffe, he made his debut for the county at the age of 17. Though run out for a duck in his first innings, he gave early signs of his prodigious powers of concentration when he scored 196, first in and last out, at Worcester in that same season and was marked down as one with a bright future. The talent, housed in a frame that was never robust, took a while to blossom. The summer of 1937 marked his transition to international ranks, and experience gained from opening the Yorkshire innings with Sutcliffe can have done him no harm. Ten centuries that year included one in his second Test against New Zealand (his first appearance for England had brought only 0 and 1), but his batting was on occasions criticised for its caution. It was, however, acknowledged that he possessed a full and attractive range of strokes, notably the cover drive.

LEN HUTTON

Hutton at the Oval in 1938: a youthful living legend.

Hutton had presaged his historic innings at the Oval by scoring a century in his first match against Australia, at Trent Bridge in 1938. The 364, through the intervals of which he was nursed by his Yorkshire senior Hedley Verity — a fresh shirt and a cup of tea or a sandwich in the breaks and a visit to the seaside, including some beach cricket, on the Sunday — subjected an essentially shy and retiring man to misgivings about sudden fame and its attendant pressures: his subsequent achievements, buoyed up by a twinkling sense of humour and a steely determination, helped him to cope with the burdens. Hutton suffered a grievous physical blow during the war: in 1941, while serving as an army PT instructor, he fractured his left arm when a mat slipped. After two bone-grafts and eighteen months in hospital he was left with that arm two inches shorter than the right. It was a tribute to his supreme skill that, though he suffered discomfort in the wrist and in his legs from which the bone had been grafted and he had to remodel his technique, his ability remained of the highest class. He was a master batsman in the classical mould, equally formidable on good and bad pitches.

After the war began an opening partnership with the Lancastrian, Cyril Washbrook, that was to serve England well for five years. They were never more successful than in the fourth Test against Australia in 1948, when they put on 168 in the first innings and 129 in the second. This followed the only occasion Hutton was dropped by England after two low scores at Lord's. Until the end of his Test career in 1955 he did not miss another match for which he was available, by when he had scored 6,971 runs (average 56.67) in 79 Tests, including 19 hundreds — figures to rival the best.

He was elevated to the captaincy of England (though he never led or had the ambition to lead his county) against India in 1952 and, directing his troops shrewdly but unobtrusively, he had an outstanding record: 13 wins, six draws and only four defeats. He began with three wins against India and followed with the recapture of the Ashes in 1953 amid unforgettable scenes. Although it was also at the Oval, in 1951, that Hutton achieved the dubious distinction of being the only man to be given out obstructing the field in Tests, it was a favourite ground of his — apart from the 364 he scored three other Test centuries there, two of them doubles, and his hundredth first-class hundred. Little wonder perhaps that it was Surrey he chose as his home when he moved

LEN HUTTON

south after his retirement from cricket — though in all other respects he remained Yorkshire through and through.

The other peak of Hutton's captaincy was the 1954-55 series in Australia, when England, with Tyson as spearhead, overwhelmed Australia after losing the first Test. Hutton returned, looking forward with relish to future challenges, but the back trouble, which had begun during the South African tour of 1938-39, was producing unendurable pain. He played his last match for Yorkshire in July 1955; the knighthood in the Queen's birthday Honours the following summer was a fitting tribute to a glorious career. In the years ahead he would make perceptive comments on the game in several newspapers, as well as serving as a Test selector in 1975-77, but, a devoted family man, he would take as much pride in his son Richard's achievements for Cambridge, Yorkshire and England, as he did in his own.

L. HUTTON YORKSHIRE
BORN 23.6.1916, FULNECK, PUDSEY, YORKSHIRE

BATTING

	Matches	Innings	Not out	Runs	High score	Avg	100
Test	79	138	15	6,971	364	56.67	19
First class	513	814	91	40,140	364	55.51	129

BOWLING AND FIELDING

	Runs	Wickets	Avg	5 W/I	10 W/M	BB	Ct	St
Test	232	3	77.33	0	0	1/2	57	0
First class	5,106	173	29.51	4	1	6/76	400	0

RAY ILLINGWORTH

Don Mosey

Raymond Illingworth was the ultimate professional's professional and today, a dozen years after retirement as a player, possesses arguably the shrewdest cricket brain in the world. During the 1989 series of Tests between England and Australia he was commentating at Edgbaston while two of the current England team were sitting in front of a TV set in the dressing-room annexe. Illingworth was explaining to viewers the strategy behind the way Alderman was bowling to Tavare and the two modern practitioners looked at each other, shrugged their shoulders uncomprehendingly and sneered. Two balls later Tavare was out — exactly as Raymond had predicted.

Like his friend and contemporary in the Yorkshire side of the fifties and sixties, Brian Close, Illingworth was a product of the Bradford League and from 1963 to 1968 he was the trusted lieutenant to Close on the field. Where Close had the flair and the instinctive touch of genius, Illingworth supplied the deep thought and analytical mind. Like Close, too, he was a genuine all-rounder who completed the double in six seasons between 1957 and 1964. His greatest success as a Test cricketer came after his departure from Yorkshire to skipper Leicestershire in 1969 and when he became the England captain in that same year. Previously he had earned his place as an off-spinner who might contribute a few runs in the lower order (an understandable selectorial view with a batting order which included Boycott, Edrich, Sharpe, Denness, Fletcher, D'Oliveira and Knight). Now his batting developed both at home and abroad but it was as a tough, uncompromising captain that he made his greatest impact, winning the Ashes in Australia in 1970-71. His philosophy was entirely simple: he demanded 100 per cent fitness for duty from all his players going into a match and total commitment from every one of them while the game was in progress. He asked for nothing more than that from his less gifted players but would tolerate nothing less from the most hugely-talented.

Illingworth's move from Yorkshire to Leicestershire saddened him and excited him simultaneously — saddened because he was (and has remained) a typical Yorkshireman in his grim determination never to be bested if he could avoid it, excited because it presented a new challenge and an opportunity to put his own ideas into practice.

cricket heroes

RAY ILLINGWORTH

He arrived at Grace Road to find a team conditioned by years of non-success (Leicestershire had never won a competition of any kind) and, together with the secretary-manager Mike Turner, formed a partnership which saw the county win the Benson & Hedges Cup in 1972 (beating Yorkshire in the final!), the John Player League in 1974, the County Championship and the Benson & Hedges in 1975 and the John Player League again in 1977. Once again he applied a severely practical approach: players must be fit, they must give everything to the team effort.

Raymond started life as a medium-pace seam bowler and a better-than-average batsman, and in a Yorkshire team of the 1950s rich in individual ability but poor in team-effort he quietly learned many lessons. His logical mind told him that Bob Appleyard's ill-health must eventually leave a vacancy for an off-spin bowler and he unobtrusively set about learning a new trade. When Appleyard was finally forced to call it a day in 1958, Yorkshire had a ready-made replacement who could also bat well at No. 5 or 6 and was becoming an accomplished close-to-the-wicket fieldsman. The loss of Johnny Wardle the following year found Illingworth ready to step into his position as a specialist gulley. Raymond was ever a pragmatist.

Though he was not a prodigious spinner of the ball in the Laker mould, Raymond applied the principles of analysis of the opposition and the conditions with painstaking care. He was probably at his best when the wicket was 'dusting' on the third day of county matches but at all times he was concerned to make batsmen work for their runs. He regarded a maiden over bowled by him as a minor triumph and there would be scarcely a delivery in it which had not to be played with care. As a batsman he favoured the on side of the field but he could hit straight and, once he had made up his mind that length and/or line permitted him any liberty, he hit hard.

But it was as a cricket thinker that Illingworth is most respectfully remembered. By the sixties, he knew every experienced player in the game inside out and every new arrival — especially those with any sort of reputation, perhaps from the universities — was studied with clinical care. He had to have a weakness and Raymond would be looking for it. *He* had had to work hard for his own county place and so no-one would have it easy from him.

Similarly, to win an England cap he had to compete with men like Laker,

A genuine all-rounder, Illingworth completed the double of 1,000 runs and 100 wickets on no fewer than six occasions between 1957 and 1964.

RAY ILLINGWORTH

Titmus of Middlesex, Tattersall of Lancashire, Horton of Worcestershire and the Gloucestershire pair, Allen and Mortimore. Until he became captain he was never able to feel that he was firmly established as England's off-spinner. Throughout his entire career 'Illy' could never afford to relax. It is not difficult to see, therefore, why he had no time for those who might have more natural ability but infinitely less application.

He had a turbulent time when he returned to Yorkshire as cricket manager in 1979 and found himself immediately involved in the county's revolution headed by Geoffrey Boycott and his followers. He was appalled by the self-interest of the protagonists. Later he became a radio and TV commentator of admirable quality. The pedantic and pompous might not like his accent or, occasionally, his syntax, but no one outside the England dressing-room could fault his logic or (rarely unkind or ungenerous) appraisal of modern players.

Illingworth, who has never had any time at any stage of his life for the shyster or the poseur, was outstandingly the prime candidate when clamour grew in the mid-eighties for the appointment of a 'supremo' to select and manage the Test team. The job was offered to him in a letter from the TCCB — in terms that he found unacceptable. It was clear that a strong and uncompromising character was not what Lord's wanted, even if the rest of the country did.

Illingworth at the Oval in 1968, after it was announced that he would be leaving Yorkshire following their refusal to offer him a three- or four-year contract.

R. ILLINGWORTH YORKSHIRE AND LEICESTERSHIRE
BORN 8.6.32, PUDSEY, YORKSHIRE

BATTING

	Matches	Innings	Not out	Runs	High score	Avg	100
Test	61	90	11	1,836	113	23.24	2
First class	787	1,073	213	24,134	162	28.06	22

BOWLING AND FIELDING

	Runs	Wickets	Avg	5 W/I	10 W/M	BB	Ct	St
Test	3,807	122	31.20	3	0	6/29	45	0
First class	42,023	2,072	20.28	104	11	9/42	446	0

cricket heroes

DOUGLAS JARDINE

Tony Pawson

The first book the Cricket Writers Club produced in 1958 was entitled *Cricket Heroes*. In the introduction Ian Peebles wrote: "Every man should have his heroes. But the very man who shines in the eyes of one may be poison and anathema to another, though in the world of cricket, with which we are concerned, this is unlikely." That last sentence did not hold good when there was a repeat production 25 years later and I was one of the twenty contributors. For I took as my hero the most reviled man in cricket history, Douglas Robert Jardine — for whose courage, determination, and tactical astuteness I have an unbounded admiration. But cricket mythology concocted by men of lesser principle and conviction has portrayed him as a villain, the man who deserved to lose a Dominion rather than win a Test series in Australia by the use of fast leg-theory. What a hard life the English cricket authorities give their captains, with David Gower pilloried and disowned for losing four Tests, Jardine for winning them!

The 'bodyline' series was central to Jardine's cricket career and the quality of the man has to be judged from that momentous tour and the subsequent visit of the West Indies to England. But how had his earlier cricket experience shaped him for so big a responsibility, so controversial a role? Born on 23rd October 1900 he was playing against future Test cricketers at an early age. His preparatory school was Horris Hill near Newbury and their records show him as bowled for a duck by a certain G. O. Allen playing for Summerfields. His main formative years were at Winchester College, where his batting ability and his personality ensured he captained the side.

Gerry Dicker, the keeper of the Wykehamist records, played with him there and recalls him as mature and determined even in his school days: "He was never young. He had a confidence and self-sufficiency beyond his years. As captain of Lords (the Winchester XI) he went his own way and argued down such eminent cricket masters as Harry Altham and Rockley Wilson." That independence of spirit, that courage to take decisions and follow them through made him a fine leader, so there was victory over Eton in 1919 as a culmination of his year as captain, in which his batting skills were clear enough and at that stage his bowling was also a useful asset.

DOUGLAS JARDINE

At Oxford, Jardine was not always at his best, hampered by injury and an addiction to work which was characteristic of his determination to succeed at whatever he undertook, rather than an indication of academic interest. He made little contribution as Oxford lost the 1921 Varsity match by an innings. He did however score two centuries that season and averaged 46.25 in all matches for Oxford, as well as scoring over 1,000 runs and playing for Surrey in the vacation.

Jardine was the leading batsman of 1927 with an average of 91.

With Surrey, Jardine's batting steadily developed. He had a long reach, stood ramrod straight and played with text-book correctness. Combined with his formidable concentration this made him the leading first-class batsman in 1927 with an outstanding average of 91. He was an ideal man to go in anywhere in the first four since he was a fine player of fast bowling, able to score rapidly at need, but by inclination a long innings anchor man. Batting of that quality won him a Test place against West Indies the following year. In his two matches he averaged 52.50 with a top score of 83 run out as contribution to an innings victory. Success against the West Indies, who had yet to become a major force, was followed by selection for all five Tests in the winter tour of Australia. His determined batting there contributed to victory in the first four and a decisive Ashes win.

In that series he played a minor role compared to Hammond, but how useful he was became apparent when their massive partnership set up a narrow victory in the fourth Test. England was struggling after losing two quick second innings wickets when Jardine and Hammond added 262, a record third wicket partnership of which his share was 98. How valuable that proved as England won by just 12 runs. That tour established Jardine as a true Test player at a time when England had a wealth of great batsmen. His turn came to captain the Test side after the happy-go-lucky Percy Chapman had lost out to the Australians in general and a rampant Bradman in particular in 1930. Jardine's induction was easy enough, winning a series against New Zealand and a Test against India in 1932 which set him up for the all-important tour of Australia.

Jardine felt the 1930 series had been lost partly because of the cavalier attitude of the charismatic Chapman and partly because of the dominance of Bradman, whose demoralisation of England's attack had climaxed in that 334 at Leeds. So he complied with his instructions to win in Australia by

c r i c k e t   h e r o e s

approaching the tour with intense determination and by making a deep study of Bradman's batting. Apart from his dislike of sticky wickets, Bradman's only observed weakness was against fast bowling when the ball was lifting. So the plan for an attack based on fast leg-theory was born. The leg-theory of an inner and outer ring of catchers was not unknown, but had never been tried at the pace of Larwood and Voce. It proved deadly to Australian batsmen and bruised some of their egos as well as their bodies.

With extraordinary interest in both countries in that Test series the Australian complaints of bad sportsmanship came near to causing a diplomatic crisis, though the cricket authorities at least refuted that charge and supported Jardine... until the series was decisively won. Viewed at this distance it is clear that even Larwood and Voce posed much less physical threat with their leg-theory than the likes of Lillee and Thomson or a dozen West Indian bowlers from Marshall to Ambrose.

The worst that happened to Australians was Woodfull twice hit over the heart — but when shuffling across his wicket as Larwood, with the new ball, bowled to an orthodox slip field. Oldfield was the only one seriously hurt when he mistimed a hook and immediately acknowledged the fault as his when he was struck on the right temple. The right temple? Yes, even Larwood was slowed by toned-down wickets and by balls which soon went soft, and there was Oldfield completing his stroke *before* the ball arrived. That Jardine's prime aim was to take wickets, rather than to intimidate, is obvious from his field placings. No bowler could afford a split field on those placid pitches, but while the shine was on and the ball still at its bounciest, Jardine attacked the off-stump with a field to match, aiming for slip or wicket catches rather than trying to intimidate when it was easiest to do so.

The unfair vilification of Jardine was still apparent in the reaction when it was thought that a film *The Bodyline Series* was being planned as a sequel to *Chariots of Fire*. Clearly Jardine was to be cast as the villain and many were busy trying to tell stories to his discredit, including two Old Wykehamist MPs Iain Sproat and Douglas Jay. In an introduction to his *Cricketers Who's Who* Sproat concocted some terminological inexactitudes about him, including a story that when Jardine's C house was beaten by one run in a final at Winchester he went to the scorebox and added a 2, declared his team the

DOUGLAS JARDINE

winners and had the scorers beaten. He was then supposed to have put up a list of his winning team which read D. R. Jardine and W. M. Leggatt and nine others who contributed nothing. A simple check of the records showed that he had never played in any such house final, never lost or won any house match by one run and as a junior to Leggatt was never his house captain.

Similar inaccuracies were rife when the 'bodyline' film was finally produced by the Australians — as one of those pseudo-documentary dramas in which fiction can so easily masquerade as fact. It was good drama, but much of it was indeed fiction. That film showed the sporting and tight-lipped Australians declining to retaliate in kind. Their main problem, of course, was that they lacked bowlers of the calibre of Larwood and Voce, but they did have a retaliatory attempt in the final Test by bringing in H. H. Alexander to fling down bouncers. He ended with one for plenty and a very healthy respect for Jardine. As he said later on TV: "I hit him on the knuckles, I hit him in the chest, I hit him in the groin, but he didn't squeal or flinch."

Jardine never asked of opponents anything he would not face himself. That was clear enough in his best ever Test innings the following summer against the West Indies' fearsome fast bowlers Martindale and Constantine. The *Wisden* writer deplored the use of fast leg-theory in that game although admitting it was perfectly fair and legitimate under the rules. But this was his view of Jardine's 127:

"The game at Lord's had passed off without any of the fast leg-theory bowling which caused such trouble in Australia the previous winter. At Manchester, however, we saw a lot of it. Jardine himself had to bear the brunt of this form of bowling. Both Martindale and Constantine directed it at him with unflagging zeal and it was to the great credit of the England captain that he played it better than any other player in the world could have done while putting together his first Test century. Jardine showed it was possible to meet it without suffering physical injury or getting out." Despite that demonstration it was 'placate the Aussies' time in 1934, with Jardine relegated to writing on a lost series for which neither Voce nor Larwood were considered for selection.

His detractors have had their say long enough. Let the man who played ten Tests against Australia and was eight times on the winning side, who captained in eleven Tests and lost only one, who scored 35 first-class centuries and who

c r i c k e t   h e r o e s

DOUGLAS JARDINE

was a tactically astute captain give his own reasoned view of that tour. In his foreword to Larwood's book *Bodyline?* Jardine had this to say: "It is curious to think that had you been playing for Australia you would have been the most popular man there! As it is I gather you were not even permitted to depart unmolested. No bowler has had to contend with more than fell to your lot, or 'stuck it' more magnificently — and by the same token no bowler can show a fairer, finer or more convincing record. More than half the 33 wickets you took in the Test matches were clean bowled or its equivalent lbw — 18 to be exact. If this isn't bowling at the wicket I don't know what is."

Larwood himself continued that theme posing the question: "Would you Australian spectators have behaved in similar outrageous fashion to me had I been Tim Wall bowling for Australia?" History soon supplied the answer as their crowds bayed for blood, and got it — to the chant of "Ashes to ashes, dust to dust, if Thomson don't get ya, Lillee must." In the present parlous state of English cricket a captain of Jardine's strength of character would be very welcome, as would a batsman of his relentlessly straight bat and classical strokes.

One of the best cricketing brains of the day, Percy Fender, whose own captaincy talents were insufficiently honoured because of his low esteem for the cricket authorities, wrote of the "climb down" which put Jardine, Voce and Larwood out of Test cricket against Australia: "It was a tragedy as great in sport as I have ever known. I don't think the Australians would have been so conciliatory had it been the other way round." How right he was!

Jardine steers the ball wide of the slips against the Indian tourists in 1936.

D. R. JARDINE SURREY
BORN 23.10.1900, BOMBAY, INDIA

BATTING

	Matches	Innings	Not out	Runs	High score	Avg	100
Test	22	33	6	1,296	127	48.00	1
First class	262	378	61	14,848	214	46.83	35

BOWLING AND FIELDING

	Runs	Wickets	Avg	5 W/I	10 W/M	BB	Ct	St
Test	10	0	0	0	0	—	26	0
First class	1,493	48	31.10	1	0	6/28	188	0

c r i c k e t   h e r o e s

GILBERT JESSOP

David Foot

Jack Board had been a gardener before Mrs Grace gave him £2 and told him how to find his way to Lord's. He'd never been to London before. That exploratory journey, to his astonishment, opened up a new career for him: he became one of Gloucestershire's finest wicket keepers and played six times for his country. But the contemplative onion-patch philosophy, full of unworldly charm, stayed with him. When he went to Hove in 1903 to play against Sussex, he couldn't contain himself. "Well I'm buggered, Mr Jessop. You do make I feel I should go back to me hoe."

No-one ever suggested Jack was any slouch with a bat. He had taken 200 off Somerset in a Bank Holiday match. At Hove he scored 71 at a rate which was attractively brisk. Gilbert Jessop amassed the bulk of the others in the stand of 320. His innings of 286 took him just under three hours and was his highest.

There are dozens of unconfirmed reports from Cotswold country and the rustic byways of south Gloucestershire about his miraculous deeds with the heavy blade and frenetic approach that he favoured. For his county, he went to Harrogate in 1897 and reached his hundred in forty minutes. The Yorkshire purists sniffed and exchanged uneasy glances as if an act of sacrilege had been committed. He simply didn't play it by the manual. And, for heaven's sake, he didn't stand like a batsman at the wicket.

A nation came to call him The Croucher and he hated it. Some dared to call him a slogger — and that was palpably untrue. He was never that. His range of shots was fearlessly unfurled. They were garnished with audacity, verging if necessary on the unorthodox. They were rarely if ever ugly; the eyes never strayed from the ball in the optimistic fervour of the congenital slogger.

Seven times in the first class game he reached his century in 55 minutes or less. It is a fallacy to imply that his frantic rate of scoring was achieved by a propensity to belt, hard and high, every ball in sight. There was power, of course: the forearms were thick and the wrists solid. But he scored so quickly because of the sheer rapidity of his shots. He wasted nothing. If the ball was within range, it was dispatched.

No bowler's reputation mentally perplexed him. He made Rhodes look impotent at times. He brought Somerset's gifted and underrated Braund almost

GILBERT JESSOP

Gilbert Jessop as portrayed by Spy in 1901.

to the point of tears, agonising over whether he was in danger of losing the dexterous art of leg spin. Unlike so many of the big hitters, he didn't confine his ferocity to the slow bowlers. He was actually prepared to go down the wicket to the speed merchants. The charge was often predetermined. He relied on the eyes and the nimble footwork — and told himself, perhaps unwisely, that he could pivot and scramble back to his crease if necessary.

There had to be flaws. He was ensnared by canny bowlers who read his thoughts and varied their line. Jessop was stumped 66 times and it should have been more. His impatience caused him to play over the top early on. The disguised slower ball occasionally led to visible confusion and an almost comically gentle catch.

Jessop was an unassuming man. The self-effacement never became mannered; he quietly knew his value and savoured the cheers of a packed crowd as he repeatedly eluded the ring of boundary fielders, challengingly placed to cut off the fours which he was apt to compile unabatedly in every conceivable arc from the crease. But he was also embarrassed when people continued — they still do — to call the Oval Test of 1902 'Jessop's Match'.

It was, of course. England needed 263 to beat the Australians on a difficult wicket. They were 48 for 5 when he went in. In the next 77 minutes he scored 104; England went on to win by one wicket. Hirst and Rhodes ensured the wonderful finish. As for Jessop, C. B. Fry was in no doubt at all: "The greatest innings in cricket." The Croucher was engagingly dismissive about his enthralling contribution: "Trumper very nearly caught me in the deep."

He played 18 times for his country, the first occasion chosen for his bowling. It was whippy and inclined to be short-pitched. Leveson Gower carried the bruises for weeks after the varsity match of 1896. Wicket keepers also had a difficult time of it. But Jessop was later troubled by his back and some general ill health, and the pace of his bowling noticeably lessened. He still took nearly 900 wickets.

His only major tour, to Australia under MacLaren in 1911-12, was hardly a personal success. He was a rotten sailor and maybe never quite got over the voyage. The wickets out there were also probably too fast for his liking. He impressed everyone with his fielding, was a good mixer, played some impromptu soccer with surprising skill, and found a wife on the journey home.

c r i c k e t   h e r o e s

GILBERT JESSOP

The Croucher lacked the family affluence of many of the amateurs of his day. Journalism increasingly became a source of income. He reported Test matches for the *Daily Mail*. If the *Daily Sketch* or the *Daily Mirror* wanted a timely opinion on the state of the game, Jessop was their man. He wrote with authority and at times with humour. He loved playing with words, working puns into his articles. An after dinner speech of his was usually spiced with a few jokes. He was a man without malice; conversely one or two influential cricketers harboured grievances of his fiery Cambridge bowling, and disparaged his rumbustious style of batsmanship. The game has always been saddled with the spite of the small-minded. His ideas on how cricket could be improved as a game were sound and progressive. He hated draws as much as his old adversary and friend Sammy Woods did.

It's impossible to make comparisons. Learie Constantine is a favourite but the statistics vary so much. Ian Botham, at his most expansive and uninhibited, was seen by some as a Jessopian figure. Both had the same disregard for a fine bowler's stature, yet the circumstances — and their styles — were so different. In Jessop's case, he had the benefit of few sixes.

Forget for the moment the famous Oval Test. Forget the 53 hundreds. So many of Jessop's innings were a collector's timeless cameos. They constantly mocked the supremacy of a bowler's guile. He dared — at 80 runs an hour.

G. L. JESSOP GLOUCESTERSHIRE
BORN 19.5.1874, CHELTENHAM, GLOUCESTERSHIRE

BATTING

	Matches	Innings	Not out	Runs	High score	Avg	100
Test	18	26	0	569	104	21.88	1
First class	493	855	37	26,698	286	32.63	53

BOWLING AND FIELDING

	Runs	Wickets	Avg	5 W/I	10 W/M	BB	Ct	St
Test	354	10	35.40	0	0	4/68	11	0
First class	19,904	873	22.79	41	4	8/29	463	0

cricket heroes

ALAN KNOTT

Doug Ibbotson

In the evening of a long, hot haul at Wantage Road, David Ripley, 17 years old and newly embarked on the career of wicket-keeper/batsman, was standing in a corner of the pavilion bar quietly contemplating the day's events, as yet unsure either of himself or his status among the assembled peers of Northants and Kent. He was alone and faintly self-conscious. But not for long. Allan Knott, 23 years his senior and veteran of almost 100 Tests, detached himself from the throng, approached Ripley, shook his hand and began to discuss the various aspects of their common craft. It was, ostensibly, merely a friendly chat between one professional and another but, in fact, a wonderfully executed manoeuvre typical of Knott's generous and co-operative spirit within the game he served so diligently for 21 years.

To the media and others astride the boundary, Knott represented the puckish school of English cricket; sharp-nosed and shrewd, yet superstitious. A congenial but wary sprite whose smile was apt to dissolve in defensive discretion rather than pursue a mischievous point.

Knott displaying the athleticism that was the hallmark of his wicket-keeping

Behind the stumps, however, he would pursue everything, acrobatically and aerobatically; left, right, high or low, gloved hand flicking out like a chameleon's tongue to capture the winging ball. Between times a calisthenic process of bending, stretching, arching and head-rolling ensured that the mechanism did not seize up and the coil-spring was tightly re-wound.

None of which interfered in any way with Knott's constant analysis of the batsmen's technique and preference of stroke or his penchant for conveying such intelligence to the captain and/or bowler. In the latter respect his liaison with Derek Underwood, in particular, became legend; an upward glance for a ball of generous height, a gesture towards the popping crease for a yorker. If this suggests merely a fine, clinical regard for the co-ordination of mind and matter above all else there was a third dimension in

ALAN KNOTT

Knott's calculations; a psychological safety-net suspended in the form of a large, white handkerchief from the left-hand pocket of his trousers.

This somewhat tatty talisman also accompanied Knott to the batting crease where, despite a style which owed more to applied trigonometry than classical art, it was perhaps equally superfluous. The stance was open, the bat steeply angled some way ahead of the nose and chin which, in turn, were thrust defiantly towards the bowler.

The essence of his success over the years — more than 18,000 runs at an average of almost 30 — was due largely to concentration, determination and the ability to adapt a modest repertoire of strokes, as required, to the attacking or defensive mode. Indeed his only speciality appeared to be a paddled sweep which he was wont to apply to balls that pitched virtually anywhere, provided they pitched on the appropriate length — appropriate to Knott, that is. At all events Knott produced 17 centuries, five of them in the course of a 95-match Test career which spanned the years between 1968 and 1981.

Of his most significant Test performances, two were accomplished against the formidable West Indies in the Caribbean in 1968. First, accompanied by Colin Cowdrey, he made 69 not out to elevate England from 260 for 5 to 414 — from which, after a quixotic Garfield Sobers declaration, England won. Then, in the last Test, with England one up in the series, he batted four hours for an unbeaten 73 to ensure a draw.

However, Knott's value to England, as it was to Kent, was not merely that of a supreme wicket-keeper and middle-order batsman but encompassed an infinite capacity to absorb the physical and psychological rigours of events, both on and off the field, and by example to raise the morale of his colleagues. His predisposition for health foods, 'non-toxic' beverages and exercise, though regarded by some as bordering on hypochondria, subscribed in no small way to the general amusement. But it was Knott who had the last laugh, performing as dextrously as ever to the point of retirement in his 41st year.

So much so that it seemed unthinkable that the artful dodger should depart, leaving a void in English cricket that is unlikely to be adequately filled. There have been excellent wicket-keepers, like Bob Taylor; 'keepers like Jack Russell who on occasion could bat magnificently and fine batsmen who could keep wicket like Jim Parks. But none in the post-war era were so consistently

One of Knott's 250 catches in his 95 matches for England.

ALAN KNOTT

brilliant behind the stumps while contributing so much from the crease. In Kent, where he inherited the traditional mantles of Leslie Ames and Godfrey Evans, Knott will always be revered as a true all-rounder. Elsewhere, one suspects, the memory will dwell on his first-class wicket-keeping feats — 1,211 batsmen caught, 133 stumped. But also on the chirpy, slightly eccentric character who taped together the cuffs of his shirt, wore ancient pads, used the same apparently derelict bat for years and trailed a hanky from his hip.

He will be remembered with ungrudging affection by artisan and partisan, plebeian and professional; by all who recognise and respect the sheer dedication and love of the game that underlined his achievement.

Knott made friends throughout the world of cricket. In teeming, steaming, exotic cities where he boiled the water, fastidiously picked at suspect chicken fricassee with a sterilised fork and whipped off the bails of the local batting hero. But he will be remembered, too, at Northampton's unlovely County Ground — that Coronation Street-with-grass — where, at the end of a hard and humdrum working day, he went out of his way to kindle with the embers of a distinguished career the hopes and aspirations of a fellow spirit.

Knott dives to take the catch in front of Mike Brearley to dismiss Australia's Rick McCosker at Headingley in 1977.

A. P. E. KNOTT KENT
BORN 9.4.46, BELVEDERE, KENT

BATTING

	Matches	Innings	Not out	Runs	High score	Avg	100
Test	95	149	15	4,389	135	32.75	5
First class	511	745	134	18,105	156	29.63	17

BOWLING AND FIELDING

	Runs	Wickets	Avg	5 W/I	10 W/M	BB	Ct	St
Test	0	0	0	0	0	—	250	19
First class	87	2	43.50	0	0	1/5	1,211	133

c r i c k e t   h e r o e s

JIM LAKER

Marcus Williams

Jim Laker guaranteed his place in the record books with his nineteen Australian wickets in 1956 at Old Trafford.

As with another Yorkshireman, Len Hutton, the enduring fame of Jim Laker was ensured by one colossal performance: nineteen Australian wickets for 90 runs at Old Trafford in 1956. Never had a bowler captured all ten wickets in a Test innings, let alone a further nine in the same match; nor had anyone before, or since, taken more than 17 wickets in an eleven-a-side match (or ever will?) — and, moreover, only two months previously he had claimed all ten Australian wickets in an innings playing for Surrey. Such was the impact of the feat that years afterwards, when Laker was asked whether people still talked to him about it, he would reply, with characteristic dry humour, "Only about three times a day." The immediate effect was somewhat less: driving home to London after his great day, Laker stopped at a pub in Lichfield. Though the Test highlights were on television, no one in the crowded bar recognised the perpetrator perched at the end of the bar, quietly consuming a beer and sandwiches.

Laker was born at Frizinghall in 1922 and played his early cricket for Saltaire in the Bradford League where he was more of a batsman, an aspect of his game that was to emerge, at times in critical situations, in later years. His bowling form in Army matches on matting pitches in the Middle East and for Catford after the war, when Barclays Bank posted him to South London, encouraged Surrey to specially register him in 1946. The following year he took 79 wickets to finish seventh in the national averages, earn his county cap and a place on the winter tour to West Indies, and in a team ravaged by injury Laker was the most successful bowler despite his inexperience. The powerful 1948 Australians set out to take advantage of that last factor and, though lack of spin bowling support and poor out-cricket were mainly responsible, in some influential circles Laker was largely blamed for Australia scoring 404 for three to win the Headingley Test. It may not be entirely unrelated that Laker appeared in only 46 Tests during a period when England played nearly 100. However, his tally of 193 wickets, at a lower average (21.24) than any England bowler who has taken more Test wickets, calls selection policy into question — and not only with hindsight is there surprise that Laker was overlooked for the 1950-51 and, particularly, 1954-55 tours of Australia.

c r i c k e t   h e r o e s

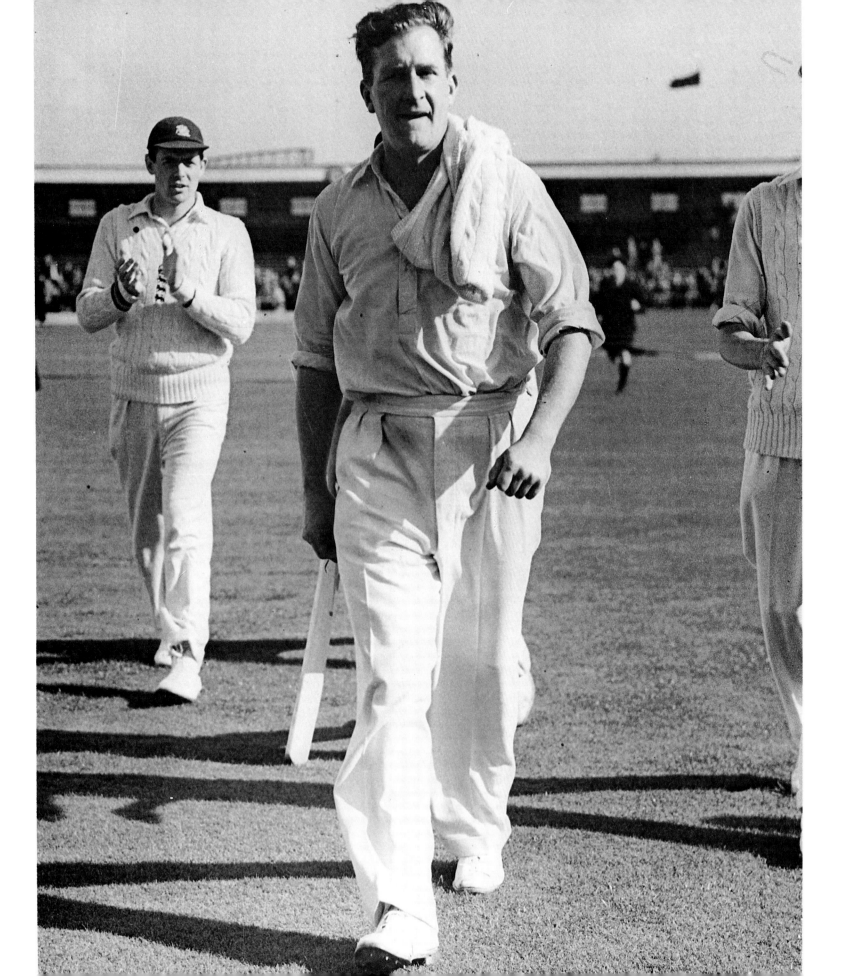

JIM LAKER

Despite being a prolific wicket-taker in county cricket (100 or more wickets in a season eleven times and four hat-tricks in the space of seven years) and returning a remarkable 14-12-2-8 in the 1950 Test trial, it was not until the final Test of 1951, only his fourth appearance in three years, that he produced a match-winning return for England with ten wickets at the Oval against South Africa. Also on his home ground, two years later, Laker and his famous spinning partner, Tony Lock, shared eleven wickets to play a prominent part in the recovery of the Ashes, fifteen more to beat the 1955 South Africans, ten against the 1956 Australians and sixteen against the 1957 West Indians. It was the alliance with Lock, Loader and Alec Bedser in a formidable attack which was instrumental in Surrey's unparalleled run of seven successive championships from 1952 to 1958. Laker was at his peak at this period, a destroyer on a turning pitch and constantly probing on easy pitches with his accuracy and variations. He was the finest off-spinner of his day and, in the minds of many, of all time. The foundation of his bowling was a perfect high, side-on delivery and to this he added mastery of flight and considerable powers of spin, stretching his fingers so widely across the seam that the index finger suffered terrible wear.

Maddocks is dismissed for two, Laker wins the Test Match and achieves immortality.

Laker's *annus mirabilis* of 1956, happily coinciding with his benefit year, was the only time he played a full five-match Test series at home and his 46 wickets, at an average of 9.60, have only once been surpassed. It has often been remarked that Lock took only one wicket in 69 overs when Laker claimed his nineteen at Old Trafford (a ground where he had previously had only eight wickets in six Tests). Laker's view was that his partner, frustrated by the lack of reward for superb bowling early on and the constant clatter of wickets at the other end, bowled faster and faster, and consequently shorter and shorter, on a pitch which was unexceptionable at the start — England made 459 by the second afternoon — and grew really difficult only as it dried on the final day. At the end of the sensational proceedings Laker indulged in a dozen polite handshakes, slung his sweater over his left

JIM LAKER

shoulder and jogged gently up the pavilion steps, content to take his greatest triumph in the same way, he said, as he accepted the failures.

Laker retired from first-class cricket in 1959 because of the arthritis in his spinning finger and caused a furore with his ghosted autobiography, *Over To Me*, in which he upset the cricket establishment. He was declared *persona non grata* at the Oval and had his honorary membership of MCC suspended, although both decisions were subsequently rescinded and he went on to serve as chairman of Surrey's cricket committee. He also reappeared as a player, briefly with Norton in the Staffordshire League, and then for Essex from 1962 to 1964. Up to the time of his untimely death in 1986 he established himself as an authoritative television commentator, whose low-key style did not often allow his humour to shine through.

Jim Laker, the finest off-spinner of his day.

J. C. LAKER SURREY AND ESSEX
BORN 9.2.22, FRIZINHALL, BRADFORD, YORKSHIRE

BATTING

	Matches	Innings	Not out	Runs	High score	Avg	100
Test	46	63	15	676	63	14.08	0
First class	450	548	108	7,304	113	16.60	2

BOWLING AND FIELDING

	Runs	Wickets	Avg	5 W/I	10 W/M	BB	Ct	St
Test	4,101	193	21.24	9	3	10/53	12	0
First class	35,791	1,944	18.41	127	32	10/53	271	0

HAROLD LARWOOD

Alan Ross

It is hard to think of a character less suited to the limelight, even less to being the centre of notorious controversy, than Harold Larwood. The main protagonist in 1932/33 of Bodyline, the bowling of fast, short-pitched balls on the line of the body to a legside field, Larwood was never more responsible than the infantryman who is ordered to go over the top. The theory was conceived by others and the orders given by the captain D. R. Jardine. In his previous Test series against England, that of 1930, Bradman had made scores of 8, 131, 254, 1, 334, 14, 232 — an average of 139.14. Larwood in that series had taken 4 for 292, and was dropped for one Test. Australia won the series.

Something needed to be done. Larwood had already played a series in Australia, that of 1928-29, when he took 18 wickets for 728 — including 6 for 32 in the first Test at Brisbane. He bowled then to a conventional fast bowler's field. Bradman averaged 66.85. At the end of the Bodyline series Bradman averaged 56, Larwood had taken 33 wickets at an average of 19.51, and England had won by four Tests to one.

Bodyline, then, could be designated, in practical terms, a success. But the feelings it aroused did great damage to the relationship between England and Australia, and Larwood himself was so upset by the criticism that he declined to play against Australia when they next appeared in England in 1934. Larwood, who had demonstrated such phenomenal speed and accuracy in carrying out instructions, was never again a Test bowler of consequence. He was obliged, as a result of the strain imposed on his left leg, to cut down his run and to bowl at nowhere near his original pace.

Neville Cardus, watching this secondary Larwood bowl in his last season, was moved to write: "Fast bowling is dying out. And Gover runs on the flat of his feet, and bowls not much faster off the pitch than the Larwood of today; Larwood who now is compelled to use the canter of compromise instead of his old lovely gallop over the earth, head down, like a young colt chafing his bit."

Cardus was rather too keen to write off the modern player. "Larwood was the last of the classical bowlers," he wrote, "he showed his left side to the batsman, as Tom Richardson did. His body swung over the right hip, and his

Harold Larwood was a true 'strike' bowler, best used in short, sharp spells.

c r i c k e t   h e r o e s

HAROLD LARWOOD

follow-through was thrilling." But Lindwall, a decade or so later, bowled with the same lovely flowing action, Bedser and Lillee showed their left shoulders to the batsman, and certainly Frank Tyson, in 1954/55, must have been as fast.

Ian Peebles has given the most evocative description of Larwood in action: "He ran about 18 yards, accelerating with controlled rhythmical strides, on the last of which his shoulders opened with a long swing of his fully extended arms. His right hand described a great arc starting from near the calf of his leg, and, at full pressure, his knuckles would touch the pitch on his follow-through. Co-ordination was perfect, so that the whole concerted effort was applied to the moment of delivery."

Larwood came from mining stock and mining country. He was rather less than medium height, but in any photograph his head was raised an inch or two by the thick shock of hair cut flat across the top. He was stocky in the manner of Fred Trueman, and he had to contend for far too much of his playing life with unresponsive, doped pitches. In the circumstances it was surprising that he lasted as long as he did, 1924-38, even though the last four seasons were at half-cock.

The last of the classical bowlers? Neville Cardus certainly thought so.

In Larwood's time, the 1920s and 30s, professional cricketers did not on the whole ask for much and they did not get much. They had, most of them, the manner and speech of countrymen. Larwood may have been exceptional, but only in his bowling. All those who knew him and played with him remarked on his unassuming character, of his domestic nature. "In cricket between the wars," Robertson-Glasgow once wrote, "the two most magnificent sights that I have seen were Hammond batting and Larwood bowling... in both these cricketers I have found something heroic, something of immortal fire, which conquers argument."

The career of Larwood, "who blew like a gale and bent the flower of Australia," Robertson-Glasgow puts as a mere eight years. It was a fact that, even more than most fast bowlers, Larwood had to be nursed. He was in the real sense a 'strike' bowler, best used in short, lethal spells. Despite the long arms and strong back the frame could only stand so much. It is not recorded that Harold Larwood had much to say outside cricket. While the Gods once lifted him to something like immortality they put him down again, gently and soon, when they had no more use for him.

HAROLD LARWOOD

So Larwood by the age of 30 had bowled his last ball in a Test match and returned to the unspectacular circuit of the county grounds. He never lost his Nottinghamshire accent, he took up shopkeeping, and he and his wife produced five daughters. The times in England were not good to him and he made the long voyage to Australia with his family. He settled peacefully in what had once been enemy territory and he spoke sometimes with visiting English cricketers who felt honoured to be able to call on him. He was, after all, the man with whose name fast bowling was synonymous.

H. LARWOOD   NOTTINGHAMSHIRE
BORN 14.11.04, NUNCARGATE, NOTTS

BATTING

	Matches	Innings	Not out	Runs	High score	Avg	100
Test	21	28	3	485	98	19.40	0
First class	361	438	72	7,290	102*	19.91	3

BOWLING AND FIELDING

	Runs	Wickets	Avg	5 W/I	10 W/M	BB	Ct	St
Test	2,212	78	28.35	4	1	6/32	15	0
First class	24,994	1,427	17.51	98	20	9/41	234	0

PETER MAY

Jack Bailey

Peter May was a product of the orthodox route to cricket fame as a player in the days when he adorned the first-class game, as an amateur captain of England and later of Surrey. Fast, true wickets at Charterhouse formed an excellent proving ground for his outstanding natural ability. George Geary, the great Leicestershire bowler, then a sympathetic and kindly coach, was there to guide where guidance was necessary. Then there was Fenner's to bat on during his Cambridge University days, those true pitches which lent added confidence to the virtually mature player who wanted to hone and burnish an already formidable technique.

By the time he played for England, first against South Africa in 1951, he was undoubtedly a player with all the trappings of potential greatness. That his quiet demeanour and classical unfussy style was matched by the temperament and determination to succeed was eloquently stated when he made a century in his first Test match appearance at Lord's. He was 21 years of age.

Already his immaculately straight bat and unerring judgement of length were in place, as was the power of his driving off front foot and back on both sides of the wicket. He thrived, especially, on the ball coming into him (much of the bowling fed this particular strength in those days) and mid-on and mid-wicket were often given, as they say, a torrid time of it.

He went on to captain the national team more often than any other Englishman before or since, leading England on 41 occasions, 35 of them in consecutive matches. He was a natural. Playing under Len Hutton immediately before he himself took over the captaincy, he learned from the master's tactical shrewdness as he had also learned from Surrey's Stuart Surridge. Surrounded for the most part by professional bowlers of the highest class and inheriting early on a fast bowling battery which still contained the likes of Tyson, Trueman and Statham, he earned his team's respect as much for the quality of his own batting performances as for the steely resolve contained within a quiet, reserved exterior.

Those of his contemporaries who played against him at the highest level are virtually unanimous in their assessment of him as the greatest English batsman whose career began post-war. For all his orthodoxy he could be impossible to

c r i c k e t   h e r o e s

PETER MAY

bowl at. He had a ghastly time once when, early in his career, Ray Lindwall bowled him an over so bewitchingly laced with movement through the air and off the seam that he reputedly played at and missed six out of six. It is said that this had a profound effect on the England selectors who that year, 1953, selected him for only two Tests against Lindsay Hassett's Australians.

Peter May back in action for Surrey at the Oval in 1961.

In the second of these, the final Test at the Oval, he went some way towards laying that bogey, although he himself was probably more satisfied inwardly when, during one encounter in Australia the following winter, it was found necessary to place three men on the cover and extra-cover boundary to him. The bowler's name? Lindwall.

Peter May's concentrated and prolific Test career came to an end in 1961 when he was barely into his thirties and, nominally at least, in his prime. He had left an indelible mark as both batsman for and captain of his country. He had taken over from the ebullient Stuart Surridge as captain of Surrey towards the end of their incredible run of seven successive championships.

Illness, marriage, the need to pursue more rigorously a career outside the game and, perhaps, a sense of disappointment at the way things were going, were all factors which must have counted in his early retirement from the first-class game.

It was a shame that the gifts of quiet charm, sensitive but firm handling of many issues, and dedication — all of which he possessed in abundance, but was not always adept at showing to the world outside — should have been given such scant regard at the end of an administrative career which he had followed in the cause of Surrey, of MCC, and of the TCCB. He was president of MCC in 1980-81 and Chairman of Selectors for several years until 1988. There must have been at least some sense of deja vu when the pack came howling for his blood at the end of his term in what had become the hottest of hot seats.

Better by far to dwell on one of the many real achievements in a fine career

c   r   i   c   k   e   t   h   e   r   o   e   s

PETER MAY

as amateur player and administrator, achievements which have caused Richie Benaud to call him the best English captain of his (Benaud's) time: "Hard as nails on the field, without ever slipping from the peaks of sportsmanship." Benaud rated him even above Len Hutton during his victorious tour of Australia in 1954-55. During the match which brought his record-breaking, match-saving stand of 411 with Colin Cowdrey against West Indies in 1957, he scored 285 while many of the pundits were crying out for a much earlier declaration than he eventually made: 295 runs ahead with only 2 hours and 20 minutes left. The fact that West Indies lurched to 72 for 7 in that brief time added fuel to the argument. But this was the first Test.

May's priority was to demolish the hold secured on England's batsmen by Ramadhin since 1950 — a grip in danger of being maintained when in England's first innings Ramadhin had taken 7 for 49 in 31 overs, before capturing the first two wickets to fall when they batted again. By the time May did declare, Ramadhin had bowled 98 overs with no further reward and he was a spent force. He took only 7 wickets for 498 in the rest of the series, won 3 - 0 by England. May's view of the long-term benefits of batting on and on in that first Test Match was justified to the hilt.

May reaches his first double century in Test cricket on his way to 285 not out against West Indies.

P. B. H. MAY SURREY
BORN 31.12.29, READING, BERKSHIRE

BATTING

	Matches	Innings	Not out	Runs	High score	Avg	100
Test	66	106	9	4,537	285*	46.77	13
First class	388	618	77	27,592	285*	51.00	85

BOWLING AND FIELDING

	Runs	Wickets	Avg	5 W/I	10 W/M	BB	Ct	St
Test	0	0	—	0	0	—	42	0
First class	49	0	—	0	0	—	282	0

COLIN MILBURN

Matthew Engel

Funny how nostalgic people get about the 1960s. It is understandable in aging rockers for whom it really was a golden age, less so in cricketers. All the time we hear how the game has declined in the past 20 years from men who retired roughly 20 years ago. But for cricket the 1960s were a devilish decade — the England team declined and so did attendances. One-day cricket was invented to try and drag spectators back into the grounds. But the young had discovered all kinds of other entertainment and the old had discovered the telly. Cricket seemed old-fashioned, which at that time was not considered a virtue.

It was an era when the game was shorter than ever of fresh characters. There was one shining exception. And he was very much a sixties cricketer. Colin Milburn first came to national attention in 1959 as a 17-year-old schoolboy when he scored a century for Durham against the Indian tourists. His cricketing career effectively ended on May 23 1969 on a county road outside Northampton when a car accident cost him his left eye. He died on February 28 1990, just as English cricket prepared to celebrate the famous Test win at Sabina Park. For his friends — everyone he knew — the day was tinged with grief. But we had all been through the sadness for Colin once before.

He was 27 when that car crashed, and he had played just nine Test matches. After a brilliant century in Karachi two months earlier it had finally become widely accepted that he belonged in the England team. In 1969 the Sunday League — a competition that might have been devised especially for Milburn's skills — had just been invented. He played only three matches and then it happened. Sometimes even now I brood and wonder why he couldn't have just had a normal accident; broken his leg or something. I wonder why it couldn't have happened to a player the game could have spared more lightly. It is an awful line of thought but the truth is that the game did need Colin more than anyone. And, cruel world, it lost him.

I'm biased of course. I grew up — if I ever did — in Northampton in the 1960s. It was a stirring era for Northampton sport. The football team went up from the Fourth to the First Division and all the way back again at a giddy rate; the rugby team was briefly the best in England; and so, almost, was the cricket team. And it had Colin Milburn. I knew him — a little.

Colin Milburn's accident at the age of 27 effectively ended his cricket career.

c r i c k e t   h e r o e s

COLIN MILBURN

He was never the most glamorous figure in sport. Even when he made that century as a 17-year-old, *Wisden* — which marked the occasion with a special editor's note — noted that he was "a well-built lad." That rapidly became all understatement. He was a fat man. It was the first thing anyone noticed about him. His annual battle to get his weight nearer 16 stone than 19 was a talking-point every April. Selectors would tut-tut, murmur something about his immobility in the field, and drop him.

In 1961, he took 43 catches, then a Northamptonshire record, almost all at helmetless short-leg. But above all, he could bat. Only one cricketer in modern times can even be compared to him: Ian Botham. They shared the same philosophy that a cricket ball, above anything else, is meant to be hit. And they were able to do it through a combination of enormous strength, quick reflexes, marvellous eyesight (though it is painful to say it) and underpinning it all, an absolutely impeccable defensive technique. In both cases, their judgments about which balls to hit were often fallible. But the ability not to hit is what turned them from being sluggers to great cricketers.

Milburn's career average, 33, tells you nothing. He had a lot of failures and I remember his angry, red-faced walk back to the old, rickety Northampton pavilion when he had failed yet again. But whenever he got to 20, he was a terrific bet to get past 70. No sane man would leave the ground while he was there, because anything was possible. In my mind's eye, I can still recall the hook and the cover drive, played with a power I swear no one else has ever matched. but I remembered the forward defensive too, played with almost exaggerated care, as if to prove himself to the doubters. There were plenty of those, not least in Northampton — where folk have always been hard to please.

Milburn played a handful of innings that will rank, for those who saw them, amongst the greatest ever played, but they nearly all came away from Northampton. The greatest of all came on the far side of the world. England had ignored him, along with D'Oliveira, for the 68-69 tour — supposedly to South Africa, eventually to Pakistan. So he went off to play for Western Australia. On a steamy day in Brisbane, he made 61 before lunch and came in moaning that he was sweating so much his gloves kept slipping. Between lunch and tea, he scored 181 — a figure that almost beggars belief — and when he was out the over after tea for 243 he apologised to his team-mates.

c r i c k e t h e r o e s

COLIN MILBURN

He was sitting on a Perth beach when he heard the news that England wanted him. He scored his second Test century on a dull pitch at Karachi and flew home with his Test match future apparently secure. But it wasn't meant to be. Perhaps his most astonishing performance of all came while he was in hospital, when he absolutely refused to let fate get him down. He smiled constantly for the cameras but the ward sister said he never did anything else in his 11 days there and the management committee mentioned him in their annual report: "His infectious good humour and indomitable spirit raised morale throughout the hospital."

Four years later, he tried a comeback, which almost worked. His medium-pace bowling was almost good enough to make him a county player, but it was never the same. The man's companionship was a tonic to the end. The memory of his golden days lives on in snatches of archive film and our own mind's eye, a reminder of how the game can sometimes be played: "Angels are bright still, though the brightest fell."

Milburn in 1974 — his medium-pace bowling was not quite good enough on its own to match county cricket standards.

C. MILBURN   NORTHAMPTONSHIRE
BORN 23.10.41, BURNOPFIELD, COUNTY DURHAM

BATTING

	Matches	Innings	Not out	Runs	High score	Avg	100
Test	9	16	2	654	139	46.71	2
First class	255	435	34	13,262	243	33.07	23

BOWLING AND FIELDING

	Runs	Wickets	Avg	5 W/I	10 W/M	BB	Ct	St
Test	0	0	—	0	0	—	7	0
First class	3,171	99	32.03	1	0	6/59	224	0

cricket heroes

CHARLIE PARKER

David Foot

Charlie Parker nearly became a golf professional like his brother Arthur. His fellow occupants of the Gloucestershire dressing room, almost all of whom held him in much affection — patently against the hierarchical trend at Lord's — implied, out of his hearing, that he'd also have made a living as a journeyman pugilist. Indeed, if the company irritated him, those restless yeoman fists were apt to be pulled aggressively from the trouser pockets of his blue serge suit.

You didn't trifle with Charlie Parker. Nor did you slight him. Plum Warner made that mistake when he came to Bristol in 1929 to speak at Gloucestershire's annual dinner. He extolled the virtues of "two great West Countrymen — I refer, of course, to young Hammond and J. C. White". He went on to praise almost everyone except Parker. The omission could hardly have been an accident. In the hotel lift later that evening, Charlie — irked by an obsequious attendant who wanted residents and guests to stand aside for the famous Mr Warner, and by the distinguished speaker's own earlier top-table insult — grabbed Plum by the scruff of the neck. Ghastly fisticuffs seemed inevitable. The hotel foyer was silent with apprehension; Warner's face was the colour of a starched table-cloth. After an eternity of silence and menace, Parker released his grip.

For years it was one of the game's unmentionable incidents. Plum pretended it had never happened. The pros heard about it at second or third hand and were not sure how much fiction had embroidered the telling. Sinfield, most delightful of men, was with Charlie that night, too; from him I authenticated the unseemly fracas in some detail and put it into print. It brought me a few coughs of disapproval. Charlie Parker was quick to anger. He was unimpressed by the social divisions of his day, especially when they intruded on his beloved game of cricket.

Yet he couldn't have been truculent all the time. His younger team-mates at Gloucestershire doted on him. Bev Lyon, his favourite captain, would never hear a word said against him. They had only one row and that was when Charlie wouldn't go along with one of his skipper's publicity ideas and fly direct to Cheltenham after being left out of the Test team. Parker could be a kindly coach, whether in the nets at Bristol or at Cranleigh. Although largely

Parker converted from medium-pace to spin bowling after the First World War.

CHARLIE PARKER

self-educated, he would regularly surprise his friends by quoting from the Bible or even, according to Grahame Parker, the classics. He was influenced by what happened in Russia in 1917 and expressed views, with articulate enthusiasm, that suggested he was a dedicated Socialist. Other cricketers whistled the popular ballads of the day; Charlie hummed instead a few bars of Beethoven.

Charles Barrington Lennard (sic) Parker was born at Prestbury, near Cheltenham, the son of a farm labourer. Their home was known locally as 'The Workhouse'. He had eight brothers and sisters, several of whom were encouraged, despite the economic restraints of the home, to study music or read good books. Hedging-and-ditching didn't appeal to the solemn-looking, thoughtful Charlie. He went briefly to the grammar school and began playing cricket, with marked success, for Prestbury and then Tewkesbury. By 1903 he had found his way to Gloucestershire, bowling left-arm at quickish medium-pace with some natural movement through the air.

Parker in 1924. He passed 200 wickets in a season five times.

By the time he had finished playing in 1935 he had taken 3,278 first-class wickets. Only Wilfred Rhodes and 'Tich' Freeman took more. He did the hat-trick six times, twice against Yorkshire and once against Middlesex in both innings. Seven times he took 15 or more wickets in a match; in 1921 he gobbled up all ten in an innings against Somerset. He was used to topping the national averages. Five times his summer's haul passed 200.

After the First World War he changed his bowling technique — and became a spinner. That was when he gradually emerged as a truly great bowler. He didn't cut down a great deal on his speed, but the grip was altered and he acquired variation and flight. On a sticky wicket he was at times quite unplayable; Charlie would have seen that as qualified praise and would have argued that he was an all-conditions spinner. The trouble was that the Test selectors didn't think so. They virtually ignored him. No-one could understand it. Could it have been, as Charlie was convinced, that Plum Warner and cricket's establishment stood between him and deserved recognition?

He played just once for England, against the Australians in 1921. It was the fourth Test, at Old Trafford. The weather was bad and the match was never completed. Charlie, who made his debut with Charlie Hallows, did nothing wrong. He bowled tidily and produced the best ball of the curtailed game to knock over Macartney's castle. That was it: Parker never played again for his

c r i c k e t   h e r o e s

CHARLIE PARKER

country. The omission of Parker for the Leeds Test in 1926, again against the Australians, remains, more than sixty years later, the classic case of the selectors taking leave of their senses.

The first two Tests had been drawn and here was a wet wicket at Leeds. Charlie was called up to join the party and everyone with even a token appreciation of what was needed approved. It was a wicket mischievously fashioned for him by the Gods. Yet, on a risible whim that had nothing remotely to do with intellect, weather conditions or current form, Macaulay was included at the last minute and Parker left out.

The Australians were well aware of Parker's reputation and feared him at Headingley. Years later, Charlie confided to friends at Bristol: "Just before the match I went into the players' toilet. Warren Bardsley was there and told me the wicket was absolutely made for me. I told him I wasn't playing. He just said, 'Bloody hell!' and couldn't wait to get back and tell the rest of the Aussie team." Criticism of the selectors was overwhelming. They in turn fidgeted in collective embarrassment and shifted responsibility to Carr. We'll never really know. Parker reckoned he had a damn good idea.

"Trouble with you, dear Charlie," Lyon would say, "is that you read too many books about the Russian Revolution. Things will change, even in cricket. But you've got to be patient." And with that Bev would pile Parker and his wide-eyed West Country team-mates into the yellow Rolls parked at the Oval. "We must celebrate beating Surrey. The Dorchester, driver!"

Parker, right, pictured with M. W. Tate of Sussex and G. G. Macaulay of Yorkshire in 1925.

C. W. PARKER GLOUCESTERSHIRE
BORN 14.10.1882, PRESTBURY, GLOUCESTERSHIRE

BATTING

	Matches	Innings	Not out	Runs	High score	Avg	100
Test	1	1	1	3	3*	—	0
First class	635	954	195	7,951	82	10.47	0

BOWLING AND FIELDING

	Runs	Wickets	Avg	5 W/I	10 W/M	BB	Ct	St
Test	32	2	16.00	0	0	2/32	0	0
First class	63,817	3,278	19.46	277	91	10/79	248	0

c r i c k e t   h e r o e s

DEREK RANDALL

Scyld Berry

If you want to open the batting for England, it would be politically wise if you did so for Yorkshire first. If you want to keep wicket for England, it would be equally wise if you began by doing so for Kent. In English cricket there are various constituencies or lobbies, based on region or social class or educational background. If you want to captain England, it is not essential to be the captain of Cambridge, but — as we might as well admit — it would help.

Derek Randall had no such influential support, and his Test career, I am sure, was the shorter because of it. He was a Retford lad, not an Oxbridge blue. He did not join Middlesex, as an ambitious middle-order batsman should, or Yorkshire, which has a strong enough lobby to forward the claims of its own. Randall joined Nottinghamshire, in the years when it was still in a state of fallen grace, led by Brian Bolus or Mike Smedley, before the advent of Clive Rice and Richard Hadlee. What is more, he was quite clearly his own man, artless, unpolitical, not given to cliques and intrigue.

In the beginning, all this did not matter. He won his England cap in 1976/7 in India and secured his place with that wonderful 174 in the Centenary Test at Melbourne. In 1977 he averaged 34 in the home series against Australia, which proved he wasn't limited to making runs abroad on pitches where the ball did not seam. Although he was dropped for the following summer, 'Arkle' came back and continued in the England side until the very end of 1979, when the lack of influential support first told against him.

In the first match of a three-Test series in Australia Randall had to open the batting — and not only open but take the first ball from Dennis Lillee, ahead of Geoffrey Boycott. He made nought and one. In the Second Test he went back to number three on a wet Sydney wicket, on which he again made nought. In the second innings he made a rather good 25, the second highest score by any of England's six specialist batsmen in the match. Which of them was dropped for the Third Test at Melbourne, the scene of Randall's finest triumph?

During his Test career, in between the omissions, Randall averaged between 32 and 33. At that level a batsman's place is not certain in the England team; he needs friends in high places to survive the bad trots. Only a batting captain like Mike Smith, or Mike Brearley, can get away with averaging less than 32.

Derek Randall hooks Dennis Lillee for four during their fascinating battle in the Centenary Test in 1977.

c r i c k e t   h e r o e s

DEREK RANDALL

Randall was out from the end of 1979 until June 1982. Allan Lamb, on the other hand, stayed in the side for four years, although his average towards the end was 32.

Of course, Randall was not a consistent run-maker. He might play a match-winning innings then fail to contribute for several Tests. Moreover, he looked inconsistent, shifting about in his crease, tugging at his cap or helmet, fidgeting with his pad and scratching around in the bowler's footmarks deliberately to annoy Lillee or Rodney Hogg ('Arkle' was not entirely without guile in his cricket). His method was high-risk, featuring as it did a tendency to play 'inside-out' by opening the face of his Gunn and Moore and re-directing the straight ball to either side of cover-point. Like a March hare, he had his moments of madness. At Sydney in 1982/3, when England had to bat out the last day, Randall was bowled by Jeff Thomson after taking two steps down the pitch and away to leg, seeking to square-drive as if it had been the final over of a one-day game.

Randall on his way to 150 against the Aussies at Sydney on the 1978/79 tour.

Dear 'Arkle'. If a length-ball from Michael Holding was going to rear, it would be Randall who took it in the face. If anyone had to bat out of position, it would be Randall first, Mike Gatting second, and never any of the others. England were short of opening batsmen when Boycott, Graham Gooch and Wayne Larkins opted to play for the South African Breweries XI and were banned for three years. In their stead, Randall and Tavare made an unlikely opening pair, yet the former still made a match-winning century in the Edgbaston Test of 1982 against Pakistan.

Surely enough, nothing so became his England career as the ending of it. In 1983/4 Randall hit two centuries against New Zealand, which would have been enough to give anyone else an extended run. Not Randall. When he moved on to Pakistan, Abdul Qadir made a monkey of him — but not only of him — in the First Test, to which Randall replied with 65 in his only innings of the second. Then in both innings of the Third he was 'sawn off' most horribly by umpiring which — as subsequent tours showed beyond all doubt — was, at times, 'bent.'

Randall was given one more Test match, a match which saw England's most naive planning since Raglan at his most reckless. To repulse the West Indian fast bowlers in the Edgbaston Test of 1984, England's selectors chose all of five

DEREK RANDALL

specialist batsmen. In came Randall at number three, again forced into too high a position by the selfishness of his colleagues. "You're sacrificing him, man!" shouted a West Indian in the crowd, "You're sacrificing him!"

The man was right. Derek Randall played out his eccentric days with Nottinghamshire and was never chosen for England again.

D. W. RANDALL NOTTINGHAMSHIRE
BORN 24.2.51, RETFORD, NOTTS

BATTING

	Matches	Innings	Not out	Runs	High score	Avg	100
Test	47	79	5	2,470	174	33.37	7
First class	427	726	68	24,740	237	37.59	44

BOWLING AND FIELDING

	Runs	Wickets	Avg	5 W/I	10 W/M	BB	Ct	St
Test	3	0	—	0	0	—	31	0
First class	386	12	32.16	0	0	3/15	315	0

K.S.RANJITSINHJI

Alan Ross

There are more varied photographs of K. S. Ranjitsinhji — His Highness the Maharajah Jam Sahib of Nawanagar — than of any other famous cricketer. But then Ranji was cricket's most various character, whose life had many parts, which the portraits illustrate. There is, first, Ranji at Cambridge, pale blue cap perched on a roundish, moustached face. Next, Ranji with a tennis racquet, tennis being a game at which he then excelled. F. S. Jackson, the Cambridge cricket captain, was puzzled by this untutored Indian and thought little of him as an undergraduate, his reputation then as much for extravagance as for games-playing. He got his Blue, but had a moderate match at Lord's, despite having engaged — in the grand manner — a series of professional coaches to bowl at him.

Ranji, though he had little money, was not shy of acting the Rajput Prince; soon he was hiring billiard markers, renting fishing rights and shoots. The pictures show him dressed for the part, now with a parrot, Popsey, on one shoulder. Popsey, already over fifty when Ranji acquired her, survived her owner, though bald, blind, and querulous. Other photographs of the time show Ranji at the wheel of his own car, the first ever to be seen in Cambridge. He is seen in fine jewelry, in immaculately tailored suits. Ranji's home State was a poor one, his grant modest. The tailors and others had to wait a long time for payment.

Ranji left Cambridge in 1894, spending that summer qualifying for Sussex, the county where his friend C. B. Fry was already installed. Ranji had played for Cambridge against Sussex at Hove and had taken a liking to the place, its Oriental flavour and Regency raffishness. It was with Sussex in 1895 that Ranji's career really blossomed. In that first season, 1895, Ranji hit four hundreds, two at Hove, two at Lord's. He was suffering from the asthma that was eventually to kill him, but he still finished third in the first-class averages, scoring 1,766 runs at an average of 50.16. Only Grace and MacLaren were above him.

From 1895 to 1904, except for 1898, which season he took off to spend in India on his way home from Australia, Ranji was one of the glories of English cricket. He hit 72 centuries — ten of them in 1896, thirteen in 1900 — mostly

K. S. Ranjitsinhji, His Highness the Maharajah Jam Sahib of Nawangar — 'Ranji'

c r i c k e t   h e r o e s

MOONSHINE'S CRICKETERS.—MR. K. S. RANJITSINHJI.

K.S.RANJITSINHJI

Spy's view of Ranji as it appeared in Vanity Fair.

for Sussex, but two of the greatest for England, 154 not out against Australia at Manchester in his first Test match, 175 against Australia at Sydney. In 1899 and 1900 he made over 3,000 runs, in 1900 hitting five double centuries. Statistics are one of the least interesting things about Ranji, but even if he had been one of the more plodding, rather than the most elegant, of players, they would have been telling.

What Ranji did, in his unique fashion, was add new dimensions to the art of batting. He turned defence into attack, substituting the forcing back stroke for the forward push, so that if the ball was well up he drove, if on a length or short he slashed it away past cover. He was a beautiful late cutter and glancer to leg, merely hastening the ball on its way by the finest of deflections. He was exceptionally light on his feet, a savager of spin bowling by his quickness down the pitch.

There is one particularly famous portrait of Ranji's stance, posed at Hove. It is relaxed and at ease, the feet at ten to two, the bat resting gently on the ground at 45 degrees. Hutton 50 years later stood in much the same way. To the same date belong the series of still pictures showing Ranji going through his repertoire: the drive to leg, the square slash, the leg glance, with feet crossed. The earliest group photographs show Ranji in his first season for Sussex, on the right of and dwarfed by the huge figure of W. L. Murdoch. Next, he is himself captain, in 1901, Fry on his left; then, in straw boater, on the *Ormuz*, Australia-bound. Now we come upon Ranji entertaining W. G. Grace, Grace carrying two golf clubs and Ranji smiling in the protection of Grace's enfolding arms. Finally the last of the cricket photographs, Ranji aged 40 at the Oval, 1912, the slim figure replaced by the heavy, middle-aged body of the ruling prince. Cardus once referred to Ranji as the "midsummer's night's dream of cricket" but after 1907, when Ranji was installed as Jam Sahib of Nawanagar, cricket took second place.

We see Ranji next in full regalia aboard an elephant on the way to his installation; Ranji, gun on his shoulder and a cheetah at his feet; Ranji, in army uniform on leave from France; Ranji among his fellow princes at Baroda, head turned sideways to hide his glass eye, the right one lost in a shooting accident. From 1907 on Ranji was less the English cricketer, more the Indian potentate. He was one of India's three representatives at the first assembly of the League

K.S.RANJITSINHJI

of Nations in Geneva, later a highly respected member of the Council of Princes. But for the last 26 years of his life his duties as Jam Sahib of Nawanagar claimed most of his attention. "The prince of a little State but the King of a great game," it was said of Ranji. It was also said of him that it was only in the company of Englishmen that he was ever happy. His loyalty to the country that gave him both fame and serenity was complete; but though he may have left his heart in England it was as a solitary, rather melancholy Indian that he had to live out his life.

K. S. RANJITSINHJI SUSSEX
BORN 10.9.1872, SARODAR, INDIA

BATTING

	Matches	Innings	Not out	Runs	High score	Avg	100
Test	15	26	4	989	175	44.95	2
First class	307	500	62	24,692	285*	56.37	72

BOWLING AND FIELDING

	Runs	Wickets	Avg	5 W/I	10 W/M	BB	Ct	St
Test	39	1	39.00	0	0	1/23	13	0
First class	4,601	133	34.59	4	0	6/53	233	0

WILFRED RHODES

Derek Hodgson

Wilfred Rhodes was 22 when he first played for England in 1898 and entered the last of his 58 Test matches in 1926, when he was 49. He bowled to W. G. Grace and to Bradman, and on those facts alone he would be remembered as one of the greatest cricketers. But his Test matches were only the diamonds in one of the richest seams of talent ever found in Yorkshire and England.

He had, as Peter Thomas pointed out, three separate careers: as a slow left arm bowler of phenomenal accuracy and patience he displaced Johnny Briggs in the England side in his second season; his batting developed so well, particularly his defensive technique, that he became Jack Hobbs's regular partner as England opening batsman in Australia; and after the Great War, when both Yorkshire and England had need for him to bowl again, in the front line, he reverted to bowling — at the age of 33 — with, astonishingly, a third of his career still to run. He was only half way through that career when he was granted his county benefit; by today's reckonings Wilfred Rhodes was entitled to ask Yorkshire for three benefits... and he would have deserved them!

As a boy, in Kirkheaton near Huddersfield, he grew up in the shadow of George Hirst, six years his senior, although both were to open the bowling for the club. Kirkheaton once dismissed Slaithwaite for 9 — Hirst 5 for 2, Rhodes 5 for 3, the four byes being explained by the scorer: "Ower stumper were reight freetened o' George Herbert." Hirst bowled quick left arm and was famous, Rhodes was another trier a long way behind the reigning left-arm monarch Bobby Peel.

But the boy was determined. He learned to bowl on a patch of grass cut by his father near their cottage. In winter, or in bad weather, he bowled in a woodshed, measuring his spin by coating one side of the ball with chalk. He found employment in the railway engine sheds at Mirfield, finishing at two o'clock on Saturday afternoons, which meant he had to run three miles to Kirkheaton in order to play in a match starting at 2.30.

One Saturday the foreman found the young Rhodes ringing the knocking-off bell at 1.30. He was sacked but, after a spell labouring, got a job as a cricket professional in Galashiels — the source of the story that Rhodes was taught to bowl in the Borders. Like any good 'pro' he had to bowl as circumstances

In a first-class career spanning over thirty years Wilfred Rhodes had the unique privilege of bowling to two of cricket's greats, W. G. Grace and Don Bradman.

WILFRED RHODES

dictated — fast, medium or slow — but the experience was valuable and he was waiting to be called up for a trial with Warwickshire when the cricket world was stunned by the news of Peel's sacking.

Even then the door was not opened for Rhodes alone — ahead of him was Albert Cordingley of Bradford. In an end-of-season trial Cordingley took 8 for 33 against the colts and 3 for 62 against the seniors, Rhodes managed only 2 for 99 against the first team. However, both were included in the party for the opening match against MCC at Lord's and tales vary as to why Rhodes won his place ahead of Cordingley — Hawke and F. S. Jackson both asserting afterwards that he was their first choice. History records that Rhodes took 6 for 33 on his debut. He was retained to play against Somerset at Bath while the unlucky Cordingley, before he could be given his chance, was recalled by telegram to attend his mother's funeral. In his absence Rhodes added match figures of 13 for 45 and a titanic career was launched.

Rhodes took 141 wickets in his first season, immediately becoming one of *Wisden*'s five. He played for England in his second season and went on to do the double of 100 wickets and 1,000 runs in a season 16 times. In 29 consecutive summers he was absent from the top twenty of the averages only four times. In his three finest summers he collected 594 victims!

His secret, according to his contemporaries, lay in his absolute command of flight. A ball bowled above the batsman's eyeline, he believed, was more difficult to play because an adjustment had to be made; his opinion on what passes for spin bowling today would be illuminating. As a young man, on the under-prepared and rarely-covered pitches of that time, he could spin the ball wickedly. As preparation improved and he had to adapt to harder pitches abroad he tended to reserve his spin for the right conditions.

Not that batsmen, especially the beginners, were ever sure as to what Wilfred was doing. He would say: "If they think it's spinning, it's spinning." The longer he played, the more information he stored to feed a sagacious brain, and his ability to tease and test a batsman by fractionally varying his length and direction became legend. Cardus thought his greatest performance was in 1903 in Sydney when Australia, on a pitch described as hard and polished, raised 500. Victor Trumper made 185 and it was said of that innings that he had three strokes for every ball. Rhodes finished with figures of 5 for 94 off 48

WILFRED RHODES

overs, many of them bowled at Trumper, who was reported to have called down the wicket after yet another maiden: "Please Wilfred, give me a little peace."

Either side of the Great War Rhodes enjoyed a lordly status — sage, guru, tactician and brilliant performer. A line of Yorkshire captains deferred to him and some of the tales told then are repeated today. A young amateur hit the first two balls he received for four whereupon his partner Rhodes walked down the pitch to remonstrate: "Ay op, lad. We doan't play this gayam for foon." He was never a boastful man, just matter-of-fact when he went into retirement and said: "Ah were niver cut and ah were niver pulled."

He spent his later years with his daughter in Bournemouth, his eyesight failing fast, appearing occasionally at Lord's on the arm of one of his great contemporaries, happy to listen to the sounds of the game, his judgements as shrewd as ever. A taciturn man in his playing days, Cardus met him again when Rhodes was 73 and was surprised to find that the old man, then blind, could not stop talking. A grateful Cardus remembered: "History came from his mouth in rivers."

It was Rhodes who first demolished and yet paradoxically reinforced one of the greatest stories in Test history. In 1902 at the Oval, England, needing 263 to beat Australia, were reduced to 48 for 5. Jessup hit a glorious 104 out of 139 in 74 minutes and 15 were wanted when last man Rhodes joined Hirst, who is supposed to have said to his Kirkheaton junior: "We'll get 'em in singles." Rhodes said afterwards that no words were exchanged. Who needed words? ... they got 'em in singles!

Rhodes poses for the camera in 1927, the year after his final appearance in a Test match.

W. RHODES YORKSHIRE
BORN 29.10.1877, KIRKHEATON, YORKSHIRE

BATTING

	Matches	Innings	Not out	Runs	High score	Avg	100
Test	58	98	21	2,325	179	30.19	2
First class	1,097	1,528	237	39,802	267*	30.83	58

BOWLING AND FIELDING

	Runs	Wickets	Avg	5 W/I	10 W/M	BB	Ct	St
Test	3,425	127	26.96	6	1	8/68	60	0
First class	69,993	4,187	16.71	287	68	9/24	764	0

cricket heroes

JOHN SNOW

Doug Ibbotson

"To be great is to be misunderstood." So wrote the American philosopher-poet, Ralph Waldo Emerson. John Augustine Snow, another philosopher-poet and also an outstanding fast bowler, may or may not have have been familiar with the quotation but, during an often controversial 16-year career with Sussex and England, he was certainly well aquainted with the sentiment.

The legacy remains. While such names as Trueman and Statham, Tyson and Willis spring readily into the popular perception, few but those who know and understand Snow, the person, can recall with certainty the exemplary achievements of Snow, the cricketer. One reason for this phenomenon is that Snow was seldom perceived to be of equable disposition either by the contemporary media-man-in-the-street or, more pertinently, by those who directed his talents. The other reason was that Snow's resentment of this misunderstanding simply exacerbated the general impasse and led to further manifestation of disinterest or discontent.

As a consequence he was frequently reprimanded and sometimes dropped — a circumstance which moved him to pen the following lines: "Standing on a still summer's day, eye watching swallows earth-hugging insect-chasing way, wondering what to do, knowing that it always happens and now it's happened to you. What not again? Yes. Feel like laughing at the fable yet not being able because you have no middle and life waits watching behind having given you the casual twiddle. Yet as your world revolved it spun you through a wider sky, opened further open eye, it's a game... "

Here is encapsulated the persona of a man who could say little but divulge a whole segment of his sincerity as opposed to some who said much, ostensibly in friendship, but who, in fact, said nothing. A man who could and did shut out the insincere who sought to invade his esoteric sanctum but who quietly confided all to those of similar mind with whom he might be less acquainted.

Thus, during his playing career, he was variously described as moody, impassive and aloof. One contemporary observed: "It is difficult to know whether there is more in him than meets the eye — or less. On a routine day at Hove nothing in him meets the eye at all. Whereas others can look merely distracted or detached, Snow manages to become non-apparent — a pale,

c r i c k e t   h e r o e s

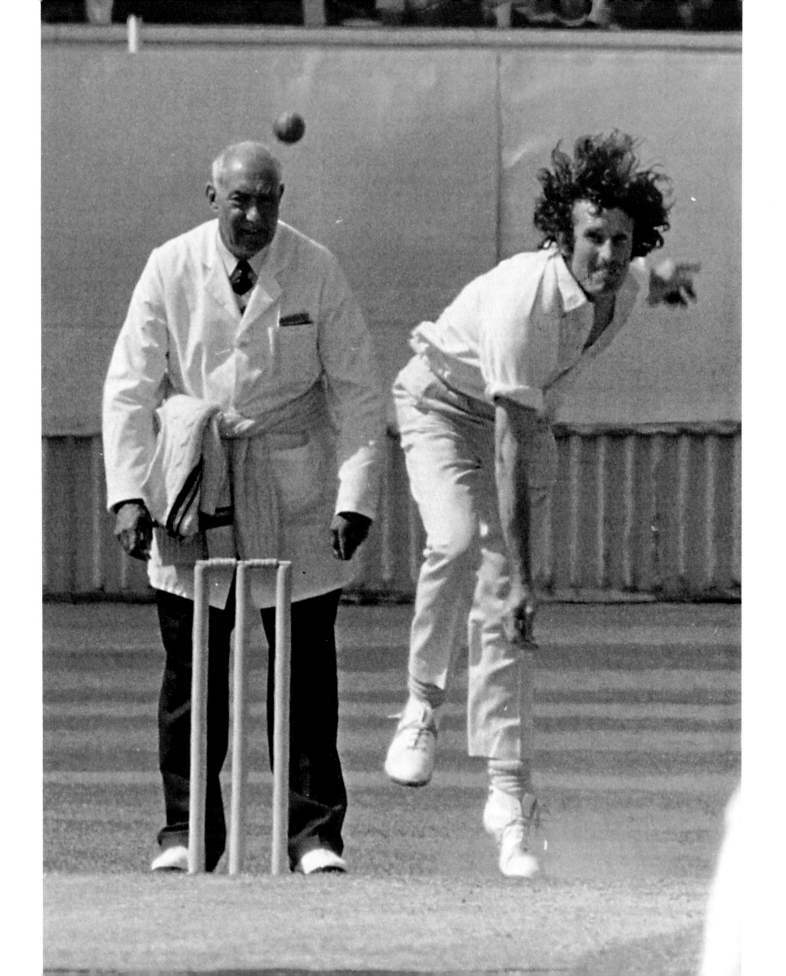

JOHN SNOW

ghostly presence going through the motions. His time-clock is one of his own adjustment which bears no relation to the needs of the captain."

Certainly Snow was not readily motivated by the mundane and generally bowled with less enthusiasm for Sussex than England, for whom in 49 Tests he captured 202 wickets at 26.66. Against world-class opposition these figures speak for themselves compared with a career return of 1,174 at 22.72 against all and (often) sundry batsmen.

Though slimly built and little more than medium height he was capable of genuine pace, delivered with a smooth, high and beautifully controlled action. His essential method was to slant the ball into the batsman and cut it sharply off the pitch. By sheer aggression rather than physical attribute he had the ability to extract lift from even the flattest surface and could produce a dangerous bouncer. If there was a flaw it was his tendency to bowl a fairly generous quota of no-balls.

It was consistent with Snow's temperament that some of his better performances for Sussex closely followed his rejection, for one reason or another, by England. For example, after being dropped during the New Zealand tour of 1969, he taunted the selectors by routing Hampshire with a match analysis of 10 for 80. He was doubtless making a particular point, too, when he produced his career-best 8 for 87 against Middlesex — at Lord's.

Perhaps the most infamous incident involving Snow's uncertain temperament occurred at Lord's in 1971 when he body-checked Sunil Gavaskar, who was running between wickets, and spread-eagled the Indian batsman on the pitch. Another disciplinary action. "What, not again? Yes..." But to dwell on such aspects is to fall into the trap that shuts out the best of Snow. Beneath the skin-deep cynicism and detachment lay an elegant personality, warmed by honest beliefs and glowing pride.

When dropped after the first Test against the West Indies in 1967/8 he knew he had bowled badly and gracefully accepted the decision. Recalled for the third Test at Sabina Park, he claimed 7 for 49 and went on to take 27 wickets in the series. It was a performance surpassed only by his magnificent bowling for Illingworth's victorious side in Australia, 1970/71. Throughout that tour, as often before, Snow strode virtually alone at the head of the strike-force, yet emerged from the Test series with 31 wickets, average 22.8.

cricket heroes

JOHN SNOW

In that same series, Snow the batsman also surpassed himself with an average of 23.50 — which was almost ten runs more per innings than he achieved in his overall career. Though it clearly did not apply on this occasion — and again to touch on his underlying commitment — as Snow recognised towards the end of his career that his bowling was marginally on the decline, the more conscientiously he applied himself to his batting which, though not of all-round quality, was undertaken with determination.

Too introspective, perhaps, to become a sporting TV personality, nor yet a best-selling man of literature, Snow initially retired from the public limelight into peripheral business to re-emerge only briefly in the late 80s as a stand-by coach for Sussex — the chiselled features and athletic bearing seemingly untouched by time.

Snow sends down another fierce delivery in the Test match against Australia at Lord's in 1975.

"So come on, who's king of the castle
now I'm the dirty rascal,
standing, on a still summer's day
eye watching swallows insect-chasing way..."

J. A. SNOW SUSSEX
BORN 13.10.41, PEOPLETON, WORCESTERSHIRE

BATTING

	Matches	Innings	Not out	Runs	High score	Avg	100
Test	49	71	14	772	73	13.54	0
First class	346	451	110	4,832	73*	14.17	0

BOWLING AND FIELDING

	Runs	Wickets	Avg	5 W/I	10 W/M	BB	Ct	St
Test	5,387	202	26.66	8	1	7/40	16	0
First class	26,675	1,174	22.72	56	9	8/87	125	0

cricket heroes

BRIAN STATHAM

Trevor Bailey

My first encounter with Brian Statham was when he and Roy Tattersall were flown out to Australia as replacements for Doug Wright and myself, who had been injured. Brian's was an intriguing selection, as he had only played in 14 Lancashire matches and had taken a mere 36 wickets. I had my doubts about sending somebody quite so inexperienced, but he had impressed Len Hutton in the Roses match and that should have been enough, because Len was an outstanding judge of players, particularly quick bowlers. In 1951 Brian was a fast medium and not the genuine fast bowler he was to become, indeed at that stage a shade slower than myself. What impressed everyone immediately was his accuracy, which was indeed to become such a feature of his bowling. Unlike most young quickies, Brian's control of line and length was exceptional, and was reflected by his finishing second in the overall bowling averages with his 11 wickets costing 20 runs apiece.

He went on to become the most accurate fast bowler I have played with, or against. He believed in that simple but effective formula which holds that when a batsman fails to make contact the ball will hit the stumps. As a result of an action that was a shade open, but suited Brian, he was a seam, rather than a swing bowler, seldom moving the ball in the air. On the other hand, his right arm was beautifully high at the moment of delivery, and chased his left arm across the body until checked by the left hip in classical fashion. He was double jointed and very supple with a graceful, athletic run up, which combined to give him a whippy delivery that made the ball nip off the pitch rather more quickly than expected. As a result his movement was into the right handed batsman, though he occasionally made one come back off the seam. Indeed, one such ball removed Jeff Stollmeyer's off stump in the Guyana Test after pitching on middle and leg.

Although averages over a short period can be untrustworthy, figures over a career cannot lie and Brian's show him to be truly a great fast bowler. In his 70 Tests, including numerous tours spread over more than a decade, he took 252 wickets at 24.84, while his total haul in his eighteen year first class career was 2,260 wickets at just over 16 apiece, underlining again his control, which also applied to his temperament. Unlike the majority of the pace bowling fraternity

Exceptional control of line and length made Brian Statham a bowler of enormous value to county and country.

BRIAN STATHAM

Statham takes his 250th wicket in Test Matches as 'Tiger' Lance of South Africa is given out lbw.

— who tend to be aggressive, not infrequently abusive, and liable to extravagant anger — Brian was entirely reliable. He never indulged in histrionics, nor provided misbehaviour headlines; he simply went on bowling fast and straight at the stumps irrespective of the conditions, which is why every captain wanted him in his side. Philosophically, he accepted bowling uphill into the wind, dropped catches, bad decisions, and 0 for plenty on a 'featherbed' with rueful smile and an occasional dry aside.

I can count on the fingers of one hand the times I have seen him ruffled. There was that occasion at Melbourne when, after taking 5 for 57, his batting colleagues surrendered and he found himself walking to the crease instead of enjoying a glass of lager and smoking a cigarette with his feet up. He also, understandably, took exception to a batsman walking down the pitch to him and once, after a West Indian batsman had been given not out caught after Fred Trueman had nearly broken his thumb, Brian produced a couple of venomous chest-tickling bouncers when he resumed his innings, which both surprised and hurt him, as Brian used the bumper as a very occasional shock ball. I often felt, that is when he was on my side, he might have employed it rather more frequently.

Endowed with a tough wiry frame and plenty of stamina, Brian was never a training enthusiast. He kept fit by bowling, rather than training in order to be fit to bowl, and he was able to manage long spells without too much strain. His ability to keep going over after over without any perceptible loss of pace or accuracy meant there was a danger of his being over bowled, but fortunately he usually recovered quickly. One occasion when this did not occur was at Lord's against South Africa in 1955 when Peter May called upon him to bowl unchanged throughout the South African second innings. He finished with 7 wickets for 39, with one of the finest examples of sustained fast bowling, which won us the match, but Brian was never really himself again that summer.

Brian was half of two immortal international bowling partnerships — Tyson and Statham and Trueman and Statham. His style of bowling, penetrating and economical, provided the ideal contrast. The unfortunate batsman trying to escape from the fire of Frank, or Fred, found himself having to play almost every ball at the other end, so it would be true to say that the success of both owed much to the tremendous and unselfish support they received from him.

BRIAN STATHAM

Over the years I have been frequently asked to compare Fred and Brian, and it is not easy. Personally, I preferred batting against Fred because he occasionally provided a loose delivery, but I felt trapped by Brian as, apart from an unintentional edge, I could never work out where a run was coming from. On the other hand, class performers like Graveney, May and Cowdrey feared Fred more, as he produced a higher percentage of unplayable deliveries. In addition, Fred was liable to swing the ball away from the bat, which usually worries highly talented players more than the one that comes in, while conversely I found it easier to cope with the ball that left the bat. Nevertheless, I welcomed the challenge of facing Brian. It always started with a friendly greeting and an enquiry about our respective families, as after the cricket, fun and laughter of five major tours we did know each other very well. Then the battle commenced. There was plenty of hostility but never animosity. The occasion I remember best was at Southchurch Park, and I remember it not because Brian took 5 for 56 in 28.3 overs, nor because I finished with an undefeated 88 on a 'green top', but because nobody at a very hectic 21st birthday party on the previous night which had continued until morning, apart from myself, appeared at the ground before tea. I think it made me keep my head down.

In addition to being a great bowler, Brian was superb outfield — fast, with a powerful, accurate throw and a lovely pair of hands — an unpredictable late order batsman, and a superb tourist. Respected and liked by everybody, he was that rarity, a man without malice.

Statham executing the perfect follow-through.

J. B. STATHAM   LANCASHIRE
BORN 17.6.30, GORTON, MANCHESTER, LANCASHIRE

BATTING

	Matches	Innings	Not out	Runs	High score	Avg	100
Test	70	87	28	675	38	11.44	0
First class	559	647	145	5,424	62	10.80	0

BOWLING AND FIELDING

	Runs	Wickets	Avg	5 W/I	10 W/M	BB	Ct	St
Test	6,261	252	24.84	9	1	7/39	28	0
First class	36,995	2,260	16.36	123	11	8/34	230	0

c r i c k e t   h e r o e s

HERBERT SUTCLIFFE

Derek Hodgson

Herbert Sutcliffe was the 'and' in two of the most famous partnerships in cricket history, as the junior partner to Jack Hobbs with England and also to Percy Holmes with Yorkshire, a position that suited his life impeccably. It could be argued that he was a stronger and more developed personality than either Hobbs or Holmes, yet he always seemed satisfied to take his own path, a man alone yet always a superb team-mate.

He came from Summerbridge, near Harrogate, in the old North Riding, in a part of Yorkshire that has always tended to think itself slightly superior — in its grey stone, sparkling water and green hills — to the wool, steel and coal of the other Ridings. His father was good enough, as an accurate medium pace bowler, to have had county trials (at the same time, unfortunately for him, as George Hirst) and it was only natural that Sutcliffe senior, when the family moved to Pudsey, should play for the famous St Lawrence club. Young Herbert lost both his parents when young but was brought up by three aunts who, knowing their duty as Yorkshire women, ensured that the boy was batting for the other Pudsey club, Britannia, by the time he was 14 years old.

Sutcliffe at the Oval in 1930, scoring another boundary for his country.

As a boy Sutcliffe was remembered for his application in practice, being willing to stay in the nets as long as someone was prepared to bowl to him. As his reputation spread, Yorkshire took an interest and Sutcliffe remembers making his debut for the Colts at 16 — "the first day I wore long trousers" — before going on to finish his first summer mixing with the professionals with an average of 35.

In the days immediately preceding the Great War it was easier to break into Fort Knox than establish a place in Yorkshire's team and, although he broke a Bradford League record in 1914 — 715 runs at an average of 47 — he was 20 years old without a definite future when the Kaiser's troops invaded Belgium.

When with the Sherwood Foresters, at York, he later confessed to taking unauthorised leave (conveniently overlooked by his commanding officer) to cycle over to Pudsey to play for St Lawrence. Despite these transgressions it is typical of Sutcliffe that he won a commission in the Green Howards and by May 1919, with Yorkshire re-building, he scored 51 for the Colts against the first team — a signal that he was ready, at 24, for greater opportunities.

c r i c k e t   h e r o e s

HERBERT SUTCLIFFE

The first of his great pairings was somewhat accidental. Holmes, like Sutcliffe, had his career delayed by the war and although they knew each other from the Colts their partnership was not established until June of that year. Holmes was 32 before he won his opportunity, starting the season with Wilfred Rhodes as his partner. Rhodes, however, was soon required to return to the bowling front-line as Yorkshire tried to close the gaps left by the deaths of Major Booth and Alonzo Drake. Although their first outing was a disaster — Holmes scoring 0 and Sutcliffe 20, having been caught on a bad Leeds pitch by Frank Woolley — at the end of that summer the pair had raised five century partnerships and each had scored five centuries.

Sutcliffe in 1934 — between 1922 and 1935 he scored more than 2,000 runs each season.

Holmes and Sutcliffe were, in fact, the principal planks in Yorkshire's 18th Championship success, both clearing 1,800 runs and being named in *Wisden*'s famous five. *Wisden*, strangely in view of their subsequent careers, thought Sutcliffe to be the more impetuous of the two right-handers whereas later it was Holmes who was regarded as the dasher.

If these words sank into Sutcliffe then it was characteristic of him to develop a defensive technique that was to remain supreme until matched by another Yorkshireman of similar resolution, Geoffrey Boycott. Not, it should be added, that Sutcliffe was often accused of stone-walling: always a fierce and powerful driver on the off-side, he also enjoyed the hook and he is still the leading six-hitter in Yorkshire's history, ten against Northamptonshire (1933), eight against Gloucestershire (1932).

Between 1922 and 1935 Sutcliffe never failed to score at least 2,000 runs a season and, although English bowling was not at its greatest in that period, he did have to face the likes of Larwood and Farnes, all pitches were uncovered once play had started and every county had at least two spinners who would be considered Test class today.

Despite the depredations of the Australians in 1921, England's selectors seemed reluctant to test Sutcliffe and it was not until 1923 that he began his second great partnership, with Hobbs, in a Test trial. They opened for England

HERBERT SUTCLIFFE

for the first time against South Africa the following summer and thus was the most famous of England's pairings forged. Sutcliffe went on to play in 54 Test matches, scoring 16 centuries and finishing with an average of 60. His career figures put him firmly among the immortals — 149 centuries, 50,138 runs at 52, a thousand or more runs in 21 summers. On the 1924-25 tour of Australia, facing an attack that included Gregory and Mailey, he had a Test aggregate of 734 and an average of 81.55!

And Sutcliffe was far, far more than just an extraordinarily talented opening batsman. A thorough professional, he always conducted himself as though an amateur. He gave to professional cricketers, wrote J. M. Kilburn "the same sort of credit-card status that Henry Cotton gave to professional golfers."

Sutcliffe could have been Yorkshire's first professional captain since Tom Emmett but, when offered the position by telegram, he courteously declined — guessing, perhaps, that his acceptance might offend players in the side senior to himself, notably Rhodes.

There seems little doubt that many of his fellow professionals regarded him as a little uppity with his sleek air, crisp whites and general air of unflappable superiority. Spectators, especially at Old Trafford, would barrack him but it was Sutcliffe's way to ignore them with the same disdain he would show to bumpers from Ted McDonald. His ability, combined with general good humour and good manners, brought him friends and admirers around the world. It is a measure of his status in the game that it is impossible to talk of opening partnerships, anywhere, without mentioning his name.

Sutcliffe's usual signal to indicate "Don't run". It helped to avoid misunderstandings with his batting partner.

H. SUTCLIFFE YORKSHIRE
BORN 24.11.1894, SUMMER BRIDGE, HARROGATE, YORKSHIRE

BATTING

	Matches	Innings	Not out	Runs	High score	Avg	100
Test	54	84	9	4,555	194	60.73	16
First class	747	1,088	123	50,138	313	51.95	149

BOWLING AND FIELDING

	Runs	Wickets	Avg	5 W/I	10 W/M	BB	Ct	St
Test	0	0	—	0	0	—	23	0
First class	527	10	52.70	0	0	2/16	469	0

c r i c k e t   h e r o e s

FRED TRUEMAN

Don Mosey

Frederick Sewards Trueman was, in my view, unarguably the greatest fast bowler this country has ever produced. No one before him, and most certainly no one since that time, has ever bowled so fast for so long and with such uncompromising hostility — 20 years at the top.

Fred was, in every fibre of his being, with every thought that flickered through his mind, the archetypal fast bowler. A grim, dour and glowering man he rarely during his career — and not very often since it ended — laughed with genuine mirth. He was (and he fostered the reputation with loving care) all about ferocity and belligerence and flat-out attack; batsmen *literally* feared him and I have seen young and inexperienced players walk out to face him white with terror. Everyone knew that the bigger the reputation of the man with the bat in his hand, the more determined FST would be to knock his head off — if he could not at first demolish his stumps. In his only slightly mellower middle age Fred has been heard to say that he never — "never in mi life" — deliberately bowled the ball with the intention of hitting the batsman. I hope no one believes it; certainly no-one who faced him, or those who watched him in his pomp and glory, would subscribe to the view.

Yet it must not be thought for one second that he merely bowled straight up and down as fast as he could. God had blessed him with a superb action, astonishing physical strength and fitness and an ability to absorb the lessons of experience. He had a natural late outswinger which, when directed around the line of the off stump, committed batsmen to a stroke and so often found the edge. He was a great believer in the use of the yorker at newly-arrived or tail-end batsmen and was absolutely convinced that he could bowl it at will. In his middle years he developed an ability to bowl the off-cutter at (naturally enough) something below white-hot pace, as the 1961 Australians learned to their cost at Headingley — five wickets for no runs in four overs. All this, allied to that basic hosility factor, made Fred an opponent who was respected in every opposition dressing room throughout the world.

Modern bowlers complain of the length of their fixture list and the travelling they have to undertake. Bowlers of Fred's day played two three-day games a week throughout the summer, often adding up (with University, MCC and

Fred Trueman at full pelt for Yorkshire at Scarborough in 1965.

FRED TRUEMAN

tourist matches) to between 34 and 38 a season and, every Tuesday and Friday evening, were to be found starting out on journeys like Middlesbrough to Swansea, Taunton to Dover, Clacton to Manchester — and all without benefit of motorways. Modern bowlers are distressingly injury-prone and complain of being tired after 400 overs in a season. Those of Fred's time bowled anything from 800 overs upwards — not only spinners, but quick men as well. 'Reserving' Test bowlers for international matches is an idea which has been floated in recent years, i.e. allowing them to rest between Tests, free from the wear and tear of county fixtures. In the Trueman era no one would have been mad enough even to contemplate the possibility of doing it. While FST was taking his 307 Test wickets he claimed another 1,745 for Yorkshire — and at the modest cost of 17.13 each. In all first-class cricket he had 2,304 victims at 18.29. In 1963 (when he was 32 years old) he took 34 Test wickets against Sir Frank Worrell's strong West Indian batting side and 74 county championship wickets at 12.84. Three years earlier he had taken 132 wickets for Yorkshire at 12.79 and, in between, slipped out 25 South Africans in Tests.

Trueman celebrates another Test wicket.

After starting life as a gauche and clumsy fieldsman he made himself into a most accomplished leg-slip and gloried in his catches there. While not capable of the almost complete ambidexterity of Brian Close, he taught himself to throw with either right or left arm and on the odd occasions when he found himself in the deep he delighted in returns to the wicket-keeper from his left hand. He shared the tail-ender's (and particularly the fast bowler's) love of batting and claimed two centuries in the 6,852 runs he scored for Yorkshire. The six over long-on brought him a lot of his runs but he could bat 'sensibly' if not quite with the polished stroke-play his fallible memory now recalls. As recently as Trent Bridge, August, 1989, as he joined most of us in bewailing another England collapse an unwary bystander inquired, "How many hundreds did *you* get for England?" Perhaps he did not understand that no-one — but no-one — has the last word with FST.

Quick as a flash came the reply: "Only one — but it were 100 not out." And that is undeniably true. For England against Young England in the Scarborough Festival of 1963, F. S. Trueman got a not-out ton. Two of the proudest moments of his life involved captaincy: he led Yorkshire to victory over the touring Australians at Sheffield in 1968 and he skippered the Players'

FRED TRUEMAN

XI against the Gentlemen at Lord's in the last ever professional versus amateur match staged there.

Ever a rumbustious and tempestuous character, his conflicts with authority at Lord's and in Yorkshire were many and have caused legends to grow, many of them distorted with the passing of time. He does, in his later years, have a rather more idealised view of his youthful personality than was, in fact, the case and he has been known to nurse a sense of grievance (real or imagined) occasionally too tenderly and too long.

But no one can ever take away from Frederick Sewards Trueman the record of having been the first man in the world to take 300 Test wickets or the fact that he was made to fight for his place by the quality of the rival candidates of his day (when far fewer Tests were played) and the prejudice of selectors who were not over-fond of his attitude or his manner. His 67 Tests were spread over 13 years and the 307 victims cost him 21.57 runs apiece. More than 20 years after his retirement something like 60 or 70 per cent of the folklore of cricket is still about Freddie Trueman.

F. S. TRUEMAN   YORKSHIRE
BORN 6.2.31, STAINTON, YORKSHIRE

BATTING

	Matches	Innings	Not out	Runs	High score	Avg	100
Test	67	85	14	981	39*	13.81	0
First class	603	713	120	9,231	104	15.56	3

BOWLING AND FIELDING

	Runs	Wickets	Avg	5 W/I	10 W/M	BB	Ct	St
Test	6,625	307	21.57	17	3	8/31	64	0
First class	42,154	2,304	18.29	126	25	8/28	439	0

cricket heroes

FRANK TYSON

Trevor Bailey

Frank Tyson was the fastest bowler I have played with, or against, and the most erudite — with a knowledge of English literature considerably larger than normally associated with a member of the fast bowling clan. There have been occasions when Wes Hall, in full flight, an occasional ball from Gilchrist, or Gordon Rorke, who broke the batting crease with his back foot, were as quick, but over a period of about five years Frank was the quickest. Although never having the opportunity to face Michael Holding and Jeff Thomson, I would place both in the super pace class.

How fast was Frank? One Sunday during the 1954-55 MCC Australian tour, when Frank was blasting out the Aussies, I went for a drive with Arthur Morris, who opened the batting against him. Not surprisingly, we discussed Frank's speed and I asked Arthur to quantify it. The England attack was opened by Frank and Brian Statham, my role being the third seamer — though I did take the new ball in Sydney, because the atmosphere assisted swing. My pace was fast medium while Brian was a genuine fast bowler, though considerably more accurate than most. Arthur reckoned that the difference in pace between Brian and myself, which was considerable and could be measured by how much deeper Godfrey Evans and the slips stood for him, was approximately the same as that which separated Frank from Brian. This was a big gap and helps to explain why Frank clean bowled so many Australian batsmen before they had commenced their downswing, sometimes with a full toss.

Frank Tyson, who, on the 1954-55 tour of Australia, surely bowled as fast as any man in history.

Another example of Frank's speed occurred years later when both of us had long departed from the international scene. Frank, who had settled in Australia where he has been a schoolmaster, broadcaster, cricket coach and author, came over here on holiday and played for the Rothman Cavaliers. During some long-forgotten match Frank bowled a few overs at Keith Fletcher, then one of the best young batsmen in the country, and I suggested that he should slip Keith a playful bouncer off what was no more than a few-pace amble up to the stumps. Afterwards, Keith said that Frank had bowled as fast as anyone he had encountered on the county circuit.

Frank reminded me of a slightly clumsy heavyweight boxer with a knockout punch, which in his case was his ability to propel a ball that could prove lethal.

FRANK TYSON

He was not a beautiful bowler and used a very powerful, rather low 'draggers' action which put a great strain on his ankle and body, which is why his career was so relatively short and why he only played in 17 Tests. His pace was derived from broad shoulders, a very strong back and the ability to bring his right arm over very quickly.

Because he gained a degree at Durham University, Frank came into the first class game later than most fast bowlers. Strangely, as exceptional pace is instantly recognisable and very valuable, he was turned down by Lancashire and joined Northants. I first encountered him at Romford in 1954, and though he bowled me out and his speed was alarming, what left the largest impression was his ultra-long, ungainly run up. He was also decidedly erratic, though his pace meant that many of his loose deliveries went unpunished. I was, in fact, surprised when he was selected for Australia, as he had only taken 78 wickets during the summer, whereas Fred Trueman, who had picked up 134 at 15 apiece was not invited, but Len Hutton appreciated the value of pure speed on Australian pitches and in their atmosphere. This was not immediately obvious, as we made the mistake, in the days when the ball did not retain its shine and seam, of going into the first Test at Brisbane with four seam bowlers — Bedser, Statham, Tyson and myself — forgot balance, ignored two high class spinners in Wardle and Appleyard, and invited the opposition to bat first.

Australia answered with 601 for 8 declared, we lost by an innings and plenty and Frank, using his long run, finished with 1 for 160 in 29 overs. However, we had noticed that in the nets Frank appeared to be just as quick and rather more accurate off an abbreviated run up. So, after that first heavy defeat, Frank employed a thirteen pace approach, which not only gave him greater control, but also took much less out of himself. It was not as if he flowed into bowl, like Mike Holding or Wes Hall, so his run-up was less important. The only thing lost was the fascinating spectacle of Frank setting off with the wicketkeeper crouching some seventy to eighty yards away. In his short approach, a somewhat laboured affair, he assumed the appearance of a cross between a Sherman tank and a Welsh front row forward in top gear, somebody to have on your side in a battle, but definitely not to be entrusted with a tray full of drinks in a delicate lounge, as the odds of him either tripping over something, or knocking into somebody were far too high.

cricket heroes

196

FRANK TYSON

In the last four Tests of the 1954-55 series Frank, using his abbreviated run up, destroyed and demoralised the Australians taking 27 wickets. It was the highlight of his career, and he never achieved comparable success again. There were several reasons. First, Frank did not swing the ball, like Fred Trueman, nor move it off the seam, like Brian Statham; his main weapon was speed. Second, most Northants pitches tended to be slow and favoured spin, and the wicket at Peterborough where he took 5 for 18 against Essex was a rare exception. Third, on a considerable number of English county pitches the accurate seamer, such as Derek Shackleton, was more effective, though less frightening, because he made the ball deviate so much more. Fourth, at the moment of release Frank's action was low, so he achieved less lift than several bowlers who were not so fast, but had higher arm actions. This also applied to his bouncer, which was easier to negotiate than Peter Loader's. Finally, and the most important reason why his haul of wickets in his eight seasons with Northants was only 525 and his appearances for England at home a handful, was recurring injury due to the strain of bowling very fast without the rhythm of a Wes Hall, or a Fred Trueman, and having to depend upon power.

It was always an experience and a challenge, batting against Frank. My tactics were to play straight and try to exploit his pace, rather than attempting to hit the ball, which brought about the downfall of so many talented Australian batsmen. I never considered a cut unless I had been in for more than an hour, as it would have been in Keith Andrew's gloves before I had completed the shot.

A fearsome sight for any batsman as Tyson unleashes the ball at full power.

F. H. TYSON   NORTHAMPTONSHIRE
BORN 6.6.30, FARNWORTH, LANCASHIRE

BATTING

	Matches	Innings	Not out	Runs	High score	Avg	100
Test	17	24	3	230	37*	10.95	0
First class	244	316	76	4,103	82	17.09	0

BOWLING AND FIELDING

	Runs	Wickets	Avg	5 W/I	10 W/M	BB	Ct	St
Test	1,411	76	18.56	4	1	7/27	4	0
First class	16,030	767	20.89	34	5	8/60	85	0

c r i c k e t   h e r o e s

DEREK UNDERWOOD

Doug Ibbotson

When Derek Leslie Underwood finally bequeathed his clinker-built boots to the Thames Lightermen in the autumn of 1987, Kent and England said farewell to a cricketer who, for 24 summers, had confounded the purists and staggered the statisticians by perfecting an unique style of bowling that defied convention, dismayed master-batsmen and enthralled a million spectators who cared not for the esoteric incongruities so long as their expectations were fulfilled. And fulfilled they invariably were.

During a first-class career which began when he was a 17-year-old stripling, Underwood claimed more than 2,450 wickets — 297 of them (average 25.83) in 86 Tests — and would undoubtedly have broken all Test records had he not been penalised for 'defecting' to World Series Cricket and, later, to South Africa.

In other ways, and not only from a statistical point of view, Underwood's fulfilment was adversely affected by administrative intervention — notably in the way the game and playing conditions were commercially tailored to fit the standard, medium-sized player and the undiscerning customer. Underwood was neither, just as he was neither a slow left-arm spinner nor a medium-pace seamer. He successfully marshalled all the bowling arts, save outright pace, and, when pitches were covered to eliminate the sticky dog — or even the damp pup — he attacked the batsman with a metronomic, mesmeric accuracy that defied, rather than invited, them to attack him. Underwood was never in the business of buying wickets.

It was part of what his critics regarded as dogma. He persisted in an over-long, flat-footed run up and a seemingly invariable attitude of delivery, too fast and too flat. But batsmen saw it — or, more pertinently, didn't see it — differently. Here was potentially dangerous subtlety skilfully disguised, for in Underwood's textbook traps were set to the half-inch and baited with a split second. And the combination could be critical. Deadly, in fact, which was the soubriquet bestowed on him by his peers and which was, in itself, an amiable antinomy.

It was true of Rocky Marciano, the awesome American heavyweight, that one could not find a kinder, more gentle spirit outside the ring nor a more

DEREK UNDERWOOD

ruthless destroyer when summoned by the sound of bell and battle. So, too, albeit with rather more finesse, it was with Underwood. Off the field, a most genial and personable chap; at high noon on the square, a fierce competitor with the mind of a Tax Inspector. That said, the intensity of purpose was seldom more than frown-deep and the fall of a wicket would invariably release an eruption of glee that revealed the inner schoolboy innocent of all but the unashamed pleasure of personal and collective achievement. And there were days when Underwood's cup of joy was frequently replenished — even when the statutes were set against him and his kind.

At Canterbury in 1984, during the match against Hampshire, overnight rain proved too much for the obligatory covers and, when play began, an ominous dark patch lay on a length. Those who had played and watched cricket only in recent years had never seen Underwood bowl in such conditions. They were to witness an unforgettable — probably unrepeatable — phenomenon. Within 90 minutes so ruthlessly had he exploited the pitch that, in 11.2 overs, he claimed 7 wickets for 21 runs as Hampshire hurtled to defeat.

All of which evoked, among those with longer memories, the final Test at the Oval in 1968 when the 20-year-old Underwood produced a match-winning 7 for 50 to square the series against Bill Lawry's Australians. Here was the young artist in his element. Heavy morning rain had flooded the outfield and, after scores of volunteers had joined the ground-staff in mopping up, only 75 minutes of play was in prospect. Australia, with five wickets in hand, seemed certain to hold out for a draw.

So began an agonising race against time that ended when, with five minutes to spare, Underwood took his fourth wicket in 27 balls. A remarkable, if not untypical performance when such conditions prevailed, but an equally valid indication of Underwood's total skill is to be found in his bowling analysis for the first Australian innings in that same match — played on a perfect pitch which yielded 494 runs for England and 324 for Australia. In taking two wickets Underwood yielded only 1.7 runs for each of his 54 overs. Such economy — and stamina— seldom deserted him.

It has to be said that the texture of Underwood's bowling had infinitely greater subtlety and variety than that of his batting which, nevertheless, shared the common denominator of unstinting application. It consisted chiefly of four

Underwood in typical pose for Kent in 1978 — his England career was interrupted after his involvement with World Series cricket but his county career continued until 1987.

c r i c k e t   h e r o e s

DEREK UNDERWOOD

strokes: the forward defensive lunge, the backfoot defensive parry, the squat, forearm pull and the hunch-shouldered punch past point.

This limited repertoire served him well enough over the years, not least when he raised an unbeaten 48 off those same Australians of 1968. Even so, it was very much with feelings of wistful regret rather than surprise that Underwood reached his fortieth year before recording his first and only century. Almost inevitably it came at the Central Ground, Hastings — now regrettably passed from the first-class scene — where, in June 1964, Underwood had enjoyed another remarkable success in achieving a career-best bowling analysis of 9 for 28.

Needless to say, the cherished century was realised in the not unfamiliar role of night-watchman — a circumstance which had always offered the best hope on two counts. First, it afforded him the time to score runs but, more importantly, the initial situation was sufficiently grave to arouse Underwood's foremost, i.e. stubborn, instincts. Accordingly, lunge by lunge, swat by swat, he clawed his way to the nineties, at which point — and only at this point — did the prospect of a maiden century begin to intrude on the principal resolution to do his best for the side. In the event both considerations were gloriously accomplished and joy was unconfined — not only among his Kent colleagues but throughout the Sussex team and the entire assembly. That is the measure of the man's popularity and esteem.

D. L. UNDERWOOD   KENT
BORN 8.6.45, BROMLEY, KENT

BATTING

	Matches	Innings	Not out	Runs	High score	Avg	100
Test	86	116	35	937	45*	11.56	0
First class	676	710	200	5,165	111	10.12	1

BOWLING AND FIELDING

	Runs	Wickets	Avg	5 W/I	10 W/M	BB	Ct	St
Test	7,674	297	25.83	17	6	8/51	44	0
First class	49,993	2,465	20.28	153	47	9/28	261	0

cricket heroes

HEDLEY VERITY

Tony Pawson

All Quiet on the Western Front ends on the note that amid the millions of victims of war just one death can be especially poignant. So it was when the news came that Captain Hedley Verity had been killed in July 1943 leading his company into attack in Sicily.

From a dominant Yorkshire team of great cricketers and characters he may well have been the greatest and best loved. Certainly he had already written his cricket epitaph in the grand manner in his final game. Yorkshire were playing at Hove when the message came through to finish the match quickly as war was imminent. Verity responded by taking 7 wickets for 9 runs in 6 overs as Sussex were hustled out for 33. That was nothing special for a man who once took 10 for 10 and averaged 173 wickets a season throughout his sadly abbreviated career.

It was fitting too that Verity had become a captain, even if an army one. For in the pre-war days when only amateurs were considered for captaincy, Douglas Jardine wrote that Verity was the ideal man to lead his country. That of course was another black mark from the establishment against Jardine, that very shrewd England captain whom they had pilloried and betrayed after he had won the bodyline series. This was the rest of Jardine's summary of the man whose slow left-arm bowling had made him second only to Larwood in the averages of those who took more than ten wickets in the 1932/33 Test series, noted for the fire and fury of the fast bowling:

"If Verity is compared with his three illustrious Yorkshire predecessors including Wilfred Rhodes I would need much convincing before awarding the palm to any of them in preference to him. In particular I venture to doubt if any bowler of his type has proved such a master on all kinds of wicket. So many slow left-handers only put on that extra 5 yards of pace when the wicket suits them, but Verity gives maximum effort all the time."

"Neither in Australia nor in England have I ever seen Verity thoroughly collared with all that that implies. He does not know what to give up trying means. He has, moreover, the unusual accomplishment of being able to change at will from over to round the wicket without any loss of accuracy. The oldest head on young shoulders in England cricket today is his. He can teach, nor is

Hedley Verity bowling for the championship-winning Yorkshire side against the Rest at the Oval in 1935.

he above learning. It is a pleasure to see him set his field and having set it to bowl to it. No captain could have a greater asset on his side than Verity. He would make a great captain himself and will yet make a lot of runs with the bat."

Control and accuracy were a main feature of his bowling as was well illustrated in that 1932/33 series. On perfect Australian wickets against the likes of Bradman and McCabe, who might have been expected to turn on him with venom as a relief from facing Larwood, Voce and Allen, he bowled 117 maidens out of his 298.2 overs in those Tests. His 5 for 33 won the 5th Test and the only Test we lost rather than won was the second when an extra fast bowler (his Yorkshire colleague Bill Bowes) was played instead.

His value as a correct and studious batsman who had modelled himself on Herbert Sutcliffe was also apparent in this series as his two partnerships of 90 or more with Paynter were crucial to the winning of the third and fourth Tests. In a later series he also emulated Rhodes by opening an innings in a Test, going in first at Adelaide and scoring 17 and 19. But what made him quite outstanding as a cricketer was the spin and lift he could put on the ball as his height of almost 6 ft was enhanced by a high classical action. He was criticised by the old school, just as Underwood was to be later, for being too mechanical and pushing the ball through too fast without the cunning flight of a Rhodes. But like Underwood he had found a style which was even more effective and economical. Rhodes, not one to throw compliments around, accepted him as a near equal. But when asked if Verity could bowl any ball he couldn't he replied: "Yes. The one that is cut for four."

There were very few of these from Verity as this dedicated student of the game rapidly absorbed the teachings of his hard Yorkshire taskmasters, Rhodes and Hirst, who ruthlessly analysed every performance. There was no praise for him for taking 7 for 26, Rhodes's only comment being that it would have been 7 for 22 but for a boundary unnecessarily conceded.

Verity was born at Headingley on 18th May 1905, but with all the talent available in Yorkshire it was relatively late before his special gifts were recognised. He played for Yeadon secondary school, progressed to Yorkshire Council cricket for Rowdon, then to the Lancashire League as professional for Accrington and then Middleton. Aged 25 he had his first half season in the

HEDLEY VERITY

county team in 1930 taking 64 wickets at 12.48 apiece. His next season was sensational for someone with so little experience. His 188 wickets at 13.52 made him one of *Wisden*'s players of the year and won him a place in two Tests against New Zealand in one of which he took 4 for 85. He also achieved in his first full season the feat which had eluded Rhodes despite playing first class cricket to the age of 52. For Verity took all 10 wickets for 36 against Warwickshire, one of many remarkable analyses which put him second in the national averages. Other striking performances were 6 for 21 and 8 for 33 against Glamorgan and 6 for 11 against Surrey. Inevitably Yorkshire won the championship, with Verity and Sutcliffe the key figures well supported by Bowes. Indeed, Bowes and Verity were to ensure such Yorkshire dominance of the thirties that only in 1934, weakened by Test calls, and 1936, did Yorkshire fail to take the title.

Verity in action for Yorkshire against Surrey at the Oval in 1937.

In all matches Verity was to take 1,956 wickets — 1,558 for Yorkshire at 13.71 apiece. In the Test cricket of the Bradman era, when many other bowlers were slaughtered, he took 144 wickets at an average of 24.37, and also 30 catches. As remarkable was his accuracy and low run rate per over. There were exceptions. The South African Herbie Cameron hit him for 30 in one over prompting wicketkeeper Wood's quote: "You had him in two minds Hedley. He didn't know whether to hit you for four or six." He was also hit for 28 in an over by an unexpected aggressor. Horace Hazell was no batsman and another member of the slow left-armers' union. Not quite as accurate as Verity, Horace was forever talking aloud urging himself to pitch the ball up, or give it more air. At the non-striker's end, listening to his chatter, I once asked: "Who is your friend, Horace?" The instant reply was: "Oh that's Harpic. Clean round the bend like me." Certainly he must have taken leave of his senses to hit Verity for four sixes and a four in one over.

Among Verity's many fine Test feats, the most memorable was that which won the second Test at Lord's to square the 1934 series. Australia were 192 for 2 overnight in reply to England's 440. But weekend rain affected the pitch and Verity became unplayable, taking 15 wickets as England won by an innings. As Jardine wrote at the time: "Verity's length was impeccable and he made the ball come back and lift so sharply that the Australians were helpless. Although the wicket certainly helped him it could not be described as 'sticky' except for

HEDLEY VERITY

one period after lunch. This result was only possible for a man possessed of such finger-spin and accuracy as Verity."

The most remarkable of all his feats, however, was that nicely symmetrical analysis of 10 for 10 in just under 20 overs, 16 of them maidens. Appropriately it was on his home pitch of Headingley. A thunderstorm affected the wicket, but at lunch Nottinghamshire were 38 for 0. Soon they were 67 all out. In the course of that extraordinary destruction Verity did the hat trick and twice took two wickets in successive balls. To rub in the quality of his performance, Holmes and Sutcliffe scored the 139 runs to win in 90 minutes with no difficulty.

After that amazing first season in 1931 everyone wondered if Verity could sustain success. He did so year after year as he and Bill Bowes swapped places at the top of the bowling averages, or as he was the key to success for England's Test teams. The truest tribute came from a craftsman with words to a craftsman with the ball. The witty Robertson Glasgow, himself no mean bowler, thus summed up the virtues of the scholarly Verity:

"Some say Verity is not a great bowler. They are wrong. I have heard such adjectives as 'good' and 'mechanical' applied to him. The first is merely inadequate, the second is true in so far that he is nearly the perfect bowling machine directed by one of the most acute brains the game has known and kept in motion, against the best batsmen, by an indomitable courage."

"His prevailing pace is slow-medium though sometimes he likes to whisk down a yorker or inswinger which is nearly fast. Only on wet or dusty wickets does he bowl at a genuinely slow pace — and then not all the time. He is a scholarly bowler, graduating to judge by his enquiring attitudes in science and experimental philosophy rather than any romantic faculty. He is tall and much stronger than his pace needs. His run-up, longer than in most of his kind, has a measured delicacy that you expect from this fastidious and neatly prim craftsman. Only his delivery has a grace which mathematics can't explain. I have seen him in certain company become rather bored with his bowling and their batting, which is something of a weakness. A fellow Yorkshire bowler says that to get the best out of Verity you have to tell him that all depends on him which argues the vanity of the artist. As a batsman he looks like Sutcliffe gone stale. That is, pretty good..."

cricket heroes

HEDLEY VERITY

To him as a person the final tribute comes from Douglas Jardine: "There will be few if any to dispute Verity's claim to be head and shoulders above the rest between the wars. No captain could have asked for a sounder counsellor or companion on and off the field or one better endowed with that sturdy equable humour untouched by failure or success. He will be missed by those who really knew him, as a man."

H. VERITY YORKSHIRE
BORN 18.5.05, HEADINGLEY, LEEDS, YORKSHIRE

BATTING

	Matches	Innings	Not out	Runs	High score	Avg	100
Test	40	44	12	669	66*	20.90	0
First class	378	416	106	5,605	101	18.08	1

BOWLING AND FIELDING

	Runs	Wickets	Avg	5 W/I	10 W/M	BB	Ct	St
Test	3,510	144	24.37	5	2	8/43	30	0
First class	29,146	1,956	14.90	164	54	10/10	269	0

cricket heroes

ARTHUR WELLARD

David Foot

Arthur Wellard was a cherished but expensive adornment to the first-class game. He lost more balls than any other cricketer. While many of his contemporaries took inordinate delight, as batsmen, in describing an artistic arc with glides and deflections, controlled pulls and carpeted drives, Arthur braced those broad Kentish shoulders and aimed for distant allotments, railway sidings (once into a passing goods wagon from where the ball was never retrieved), the River Tone and vulnerable passing traffic on adjacent roads. He did it with a deadpan expression, even though it was often a comic process. His respect for the bowler would usually be manifested with an exaggerated straight bat for the first over or so. Then, with no more than a token backlift, he proceeded to endanger circling gulls at Hove or starlings reckless enough to perch in the loftier conifers around long-on area at Weston.

He especially liked Wells, more for its short boundaries we must assume than its ecclesiastical decorum. Derbyshire's Tom Armstrong was belted for five sixes in an over and, two years later, Kent's Frank Woolley suffered a similar indignity. The crowd seemed half composed of theological students, who wisely kept one eye on the heavens as the ball kept dropping disconcertingly to earth amid a flutter of cassocks. Woolley had had enough after two overs (0-40) and retired to the outfield. Wellard also dismissed him twice leg-before in that same match; for a man of less generous nature, it would have almost looked like a vendetta.

Because cricket is such a romantic and quirky game, we tend to remember Arthur Wellard primarily for his batting, unorthodox though it was. Aged Somerset spectators still tell you they saw most of his 72 sixes in 1935 — a national record superseded by Ian Botham exactly half a century later — and momentarily, reprehensibly, forget his bowling. He was fast-medium, with a high action and a hint of a leap as he reached the wicket. The ball swung away from the right-hander or might break back wickedly. He took 1,614 wickets, a hundred wickets in a season eight times, and in 1929 did the hat-trick against Leicestershire. Arthur at one end and his devoted friend, Bill Andrews, the in-swinger, soon to be at the other — a formidable and ever-convivial new ball attack in the years running up to the war.

cricket heroes

ARTHUR WELLARD

Wellard was an all-rounder in the most comprehensive sense. Three times he did the double. And his big hands, either at slip or at silly mid-off, never failed him. He held on to 375 catches, often demonstrating an intrepid nature and, for a big easy-going man, the sharpest of reflexes. When fielding in front of the wicket on a hot afternoon, he was known to take out his false teeth and put them in his pocket. It changed his appearance markedly and the cunning old campaigner knew it. "I don't mind you standing there breathing down my shirt front, but for heaven's sake, put your bloody dentures back in," one Glamorgan skipper pleaded.

No-one is too sure how Kent let him slip away. He arrived in the West Country with what seemed like a cockney accent and the flashiest suit any of the players at Taunton had ever seen. Half the team began to hero-worship him, not only the pros. Out of season he played football; in the dressing room he played solo or poker with far too much skill for the other cricketers sheltering from the rain. He was a friendly, dry-humoured man, never garrulous. He liked a bet and would pass on a tip. If there was an evening race meeting at Bath during the festival, he'd be the first man dressed and away. After play at Bristol, he would follow the dogs at Eastville. A friend claimed Wellard had special pockets built into the fronts of his trousers. That was where he kept his notes at the races; he argued that pickpockets could too easily get at his money in a back pocket.

Wellard, a big, commanding figure with plenty of basic wisdom, was something of an elder statesman in the dressing room. He delegated Andrews to go to the secretary in search of better terms. Arthur went himself in 1948 when Gimblett had scored his 310 at Eastbourne. Brigadier Lancaster, once of the Indian Army, was then the secretary. He was a tall, erect, rather distant figure, somewhat too military in bearing for most of the professionals. "Brigadier," said Wellard, never too overawed by rank, "we've got to recognise Harold's knock, somehow or other. I think we ought to have a collection round the ground for our next home match." The idea was rejected and Wellard banged the door as he went out of the office.

Wellard would cuss at what he saw as injustice. He was wary of cricket officials with too much power and loquacious committee members who didn't really understand the game. Some of the other players could articulate the

c r i c k e t   h e r o e s

210

ARTHUR WELLARD

day's nuances better. He was an uncomplicated man who ran his thick, eloquent fingers along the seam and got on with it. By way of variation, he would adeptly turn to off spinners.

At Somerset he was the most spectacular all-rounder they had had since Sammy Woods. He dressed better than Sammy, whether it was revealed by the crease in his flannels or the polish on his shoes. He had a pride in the craft of cricket — and his pride was hurt when the county told him, with relative tact by their own standards, that it was time to go. "He walked around with his bootlaces undone, something we'd never seen before," a team-mate told me.

Arthur went into the league, where his exciting, personalised technique was immediately embraced. When into his seventies, he was offering kindly rebuke and ignoring rheumatism as he played for and umpired Harold Pinter's Gaieties. I was privileged to share the field with him in his final match, as part of Somerset's centenary celebrations at Weston's Clarence Park in 1975. He opened the bowling, the arm no longer quite at 12 o'clock, with Bill — there were moist eyes and laughter.

There was one Test against New Zealand in 1937 and one against the Aussies the following year. He would have gone to India on the 1939-40 tour but for the war. "Yet I'd already been there, old cock," he would say with mock worldliness. "Went on tour with Lord Tennyson. Hure... [the welcome West Country inflection] Did I ever tell you about that tiger shoot?" It was his favourite story. But for those who went to watch him at Taunton, Bath, Weston and Wells, every innings of Wellard's was a story worth telling.

A. W. WELLARD   SOMERSET
BORN 8.4.02, SOUTHFLEET, KENT

BATTING

	Matches	Innings	Not out	Runs	High score	Avg	100
Test	2	4	0	47	38	11.75	0
First class	417	679	46	12,485	112	19.72	2

BOWLING AND FIELDING

	Runs	Wickets	Avg	5 W/I	10 W/M	BB	Ct	St
Test	237	7	33.85	0	0	4/81	2	0
First class	39,302	1,614	24.35	108	24	8/52	375	0

cricket heroes

BOB WILLIS

Alan Lee

Since the heady days of John Snow's pomp, England has produced only one great fast bowler in virtually 20 years and to say that he was a misfit who conquered long odds is to do the case little justice. Bob Willis resembled the photofit image of the top quick bowler in neither body nor brain, yet through an intense desire to succeed he became, for a time, the most prolific English wicket-taker in the history of Test cricket. When Willis retired, at the end of the 1984 season, he had taken 325 wickets in 90 Tests. This despite serious injuries brought about by a gangling physique ill-suited to the punishing, pounding routine and, in addition, a complex, fretful personality not altogether ideal for his essentially simple role.

It must be one of the heaviest regrets of those running the England team that, for so much of his career, Willis did not have a regular partner with the new ball. It may be a cliche to say that fast bowlers hunt best in pairs but it is also undoubtedly true; the history of the game is littered with the evidence. If Willis's time had coincided with Snow's, who can say how much richer England's fortunes might have been? Sadly, after four successful liaisons on the triumphant Ashes tour of 1970-71, they didn't play together again until the fourth Test of 1976, the last of Snow's turbulent career. Injuries were partly to blame but so too were other, less persuasive factors. It amounted to a shocking waste of potentially rewarding resources. For the remainder of his career, Willis had a bewildering variety of partners. At the tail-end of the 1970s, Ian Botham's ability to swing the new ball created an effectively contrasting strike team; then, early in the 1980s, it seemed that Graham Dilley would become the hostile ally he had long sought. But Botham's bowling flagged along with Dilley's fitness and Willis ploughed a lonely furrow once more.

Not that one would have said he suffered from solitude; in other respects, he positively sought it. Willis was at his quirkiest on the eve of a big match. His nerves were legendary and they became no less of a problem for the familiarity of such occasions. He was almost ten years an England player when he began to resort to hypnotherapy to calm him and channel his motivation away from negative thoughts. He swore by the process and was influential in introducing it to other, similarly afflicted sportsmen.

Another victim for Bob Willis as Mohsin Khan of Pakistan is caught behind the wicket.

cricket heroes

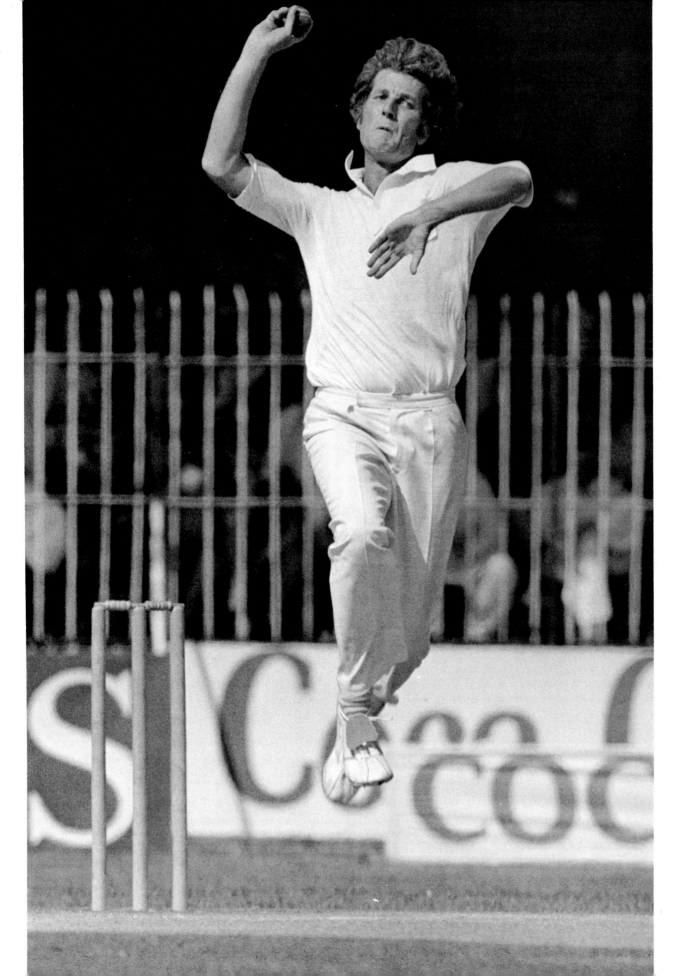

BOB WILLIS

At times of stress Willis was poor company — distracted, introverted and thoroughly gloomy. He is, however, a man of contradictions and when the pressure was off, at the end of a game or, ideally, away from cricket altogether, he was invariably the life and soul of any party, his manic sense of humour utterly infectious.

He is and always has been a lover of music, though his tastes have changed from the obsessional following for Bob Dylan which accounts for his self-added third forename, to a liking of classics and the opera. It was the rhythms and laments of Dylan which accompanied him throughout his early, tearaway years in the game and which sit comfortably with his personality. To call Willis a rebel might be to slight a man of certain reactionary views, but his opinions have always been strongly formulated and firmly aired.

It was thought that he would stay active in the game and, indeed, he set out to do so in a managerial role, first with the Young England side and then the full touring team to the Caribbean in 1986. That disastrous tour demanded scapegoats, however, and Willis suffered more than any.

Crowe of New Zealand is comprehensively beaten to give Willis his 300th Test wicket.

Just conceivably, he is happier without any direct involvement in cricket. The game certainly gave him more than his share of heartaches. In 1975, when he ought to have been approaching his peak, his knees gave out under the unnatural strain of supporting his 6 foot 6 inch frame thumping into the return crease dozens of time a day. The knees were operated upon simultaneously in April of that year and pessimists pondered his chances of ever bowling fast again. Yet he was back in action before the end of the summer and returned to the England side against the 1976 West Indians. There, occasional injury and illness aside, he was to stay until his 90th and final Test eight years later.

Along the way, he dallied with the two great temptations of the era and narrowly resisted them both. In 1977 he closely considered an offer to join Kerry Packer's World Series Cricket before ultimately rejecting it and becoming vociferous against the project. Then, in 1982, he was offered the captaincy of the unofficial English party to tour South Africa. He gave it serious thought but, as he later recalled: "I turned it down for the same reasons that I turned down World Series Cricket. I had become establishment-minded and could still not imagine being sufficiently motivated by international matches which were not what they claimed to be." With supreme irony, he was made captain of

BOB WILLIS

England two months later. It was a job he had seldom contemplated, much less coveted, despite being vice-captain on various overseas tours. He had been at home in that job, using his undoubted powers of motivation off the field and concentrating on his bowling once the game began. Perhaps he was not so effective in total charge, though he did lead England to victory in three consecutive home series, a record which would be welcomed now.

He played his final game for England at the age of 35, advanced for a fast bowler, and he was already 31 when he guaranteed his place in cricket folklore with that astonishing, match-winning spell at Headingley in 1981. Botham's century had turned the game but Willis's inspired bowling, delivered by a man who might easily have been in a trance, secured the most famous win in recent England history. If anyone has ever bowled with more obsessional intensity for England I should like to have seen it. The image of that day is how Willis will always be remembered.

Bob Willis: obsessional intensity.

R. G. D. WILLIS SURREY AND WARWICKSHIRE
BORN 30.5.49, SUNDERLAND, COUNTY DURHAM

BATTING

	Matches	Innings	Not out	Runs	High score	Avg	100
Test	90	128	55	840	28*	11.50	0
First class	308	333	145	2,690	72	14.30	0

BOWLING AND FIELDING

	Runs	Wickets	Avg	5 W/I	10 W/M	BB	Ct	St
Test	8,190	325	25.20	16	0	8/43	39	0
First class	22,468	899	24.99	34	2	8/32	134	0

FRANK WOOLLEY

○○○

E. W. Swanton

Frank Woolley's arrival at Kent coincided with the county's run of four Championships within eight seasons.

Frank Woolley was a cricketer of the Golden Age, and in particular of Kent's golden age. His arrival in 1906 and swift maturing coincided with the county's first era of supremacy wherein within eight years they won four Championships. They did so with what seems in retrospect an ideal and enviable blend of amateur and professional — and it was this combination which gives us the key to Frank's cricket. When he first blossomed as a tall, slim 19-year-old, J. T. Tyldesley was the only professional who could hold an undoubted place in the England XI as a batsman. In Kent's first Championship year the first five places in the batting averages were filled by amateurs. Brought up in the Kent nursery at Tonbridge, his birth-place, Woolley saw their glamorous style of play as a lad, and determined that in order to succeed their methods should be his.

He wasted little time. The first of his 145 hundreds, made against Hampshire a few days after his debut, fittingly at Tonbridge, took him an hour and a half. He had gone in with the score at 23 for three. From the start his batting embodied the spirit of Kent cricket as it then was; very soon he was excelling all in the attractiveness of his play, just as Jack Hobbs had begun to do for Surrey at the Oval a year earlier. How lucky it was for the game that these two superb cricketers emerged when they did, as examples to their profession — off the field, be it said, as well as on.

Frank, of course, had two strings to his bow — indeed three since his tally of 1,018 catches (mostly at slip) has never been approached. Though it is his batting which has ensured his enduring fame, he and Colin Blythe made a formidable combination of slow left-arm bowling for Kent. Both were considerable spinners of the ball, Blythe also a master of flight, his younger partner with a steep trajectory which made him specially difficult on wet pitches. He once took 10 for 54 against Australia at the Oval. Until 1923 he regularly took over 100 wickets a season and only 26 men in history have exceeded his career total of 2,068. His mountain of runs, 58,969, has been bettered only by Hobbs. Four times he scored 2,000 runs and took 100 wickets in a season. No-one else has achieved that, though George Hirst's 2,385 runs and 208 wickets stands as the unachievable peak of all-roundedness.

FRANK WOOLLEY

The art of Frank's batting was based on an eminently sound, orthodox technique. With a high back-lift and full follow-through he swung his bat through a long perpendicular arc. He had height and reach to enable him to get well over the ball when coming forward, and he used the dimensions of the crease to cover the ball when playing back. He was utterly free from mannerism and affectation. Though distinctly stiff-legged as he approached the wicket — he was sometimes known as Stalky — he was all elegance when he got there. What endeared him to the crowds and compelled their admiration to a degree scarcely paralleled was his apparently complete air of authority over all bowlers. They were all grist to his mill, and he was never known to express either preference for or aversion to anyone, be he fast or slow or neither.

If a bowler seemed a particular danger his instinct was to put him in his place. His first encounter with Hedley Verity was characteristic. Saying in effect to his partner, "This chap looks useful — leave him to me," he dealt out some particularly severe treatment. He took seven sixes, five off the useful one, and 16 fours; 188 in all in two hours and three-quarters. It was this sort of virtuoso performance that made him the dread of Kent's opponents.

Frank was the very antithesis of the calculating, bread-and-butter cricketer. He played every ball on its merits, and he was indifferent to milestones. Half a dozen men made more hundreds than he did — Hobbs 52 more — but only Hobbs made more runs. He was out in the nineties 35 times (it would need some indefatigable figure-man to claim this as an actual rather than a highly probable record). Indeed his most famous Test feat was his batting in the Lord's Test of 1921 against Australia when England otherwise had no answer to the fast bowling of Gregory and McDonald — 95 out of a total of 187 in the first innings, 93 out of 283 in the second.

Those who set much store on figures have sometimes disparaged Frank on the grounds that in his 64 Tests he averaged only 36. A closer look reveals that that Lord's occasion in 1921 when he batted at No. 3 was his 29th Test, and it was the first time he had gone in higher than No. 5. As an all-rounder it was usually No. 7 and in several cases No. 8. What is certainly relevant is that he played 15 Tests on the mat in South Africa, and on that surface he was distinctly less happy and successful. On turf no contemporary or competent critic ever challenged his supreme quality.

The unmistakeable style which brought Frank Woolley more than 58,000 runs.

FRANK WOOLLEY

Numerous innings stay clear in the mind. The 41 he made in the first hour or so of the wonderful Australian Test at Lord's in 1930 was incomparable, a gem if ever there was one. Aged 43, that was the only time he went in first for England. Two years later, however, he was sent in first at Old Trafford in a North v South Test Trial. He saw off Larwood and Voce and made 50 out of 72 in less than an hour before being caught at long-on off a full-pitch. He liked going in first in later years because he said he could see the ball better.

He did so one morning in the Canterbury Week of 1934 against Notts on a pitch made spiteful by rain. When he returned after an hour and forty minutes the board showed 155 for two, last man 101, and Notts were wringing their fingers and perhaps wondering whether they had been wise to bowl so short.

In the year of his retirement, 1938, MCC chose him as captain of the Players at Lord's. After he had been applauded all the way to the wicket Frank stood and with a gesture of simple dignity raised his cap, facing in turn the Grand Stand, the 'free seats', the Tavern side and the Pavilion. Then, taking guard, he showed in a lovely innings of 41 (and at the age of 51) how to play Kenneth Farnes, whose fast bowling (eight for 43) was described as the best seen in the match since Arthur Fielder took all ten in 1906. Frank lived to 91, forty years after he had last been seen on a Kentish field. Teenagers then were now coming up towards their sixties. Yet at the Thanksgiving Service in Canterbury Cathedral, at which Lord Cornwallis, one of his old captains, gave the address, the Quire which holds 600 was full. That was the measure of the affection and admiration that was felt within the County for its greatest cricketer.

F. E. WOOLLEY KENT
BORN 27.5.1887, TONBRIDGE, KENT

BATTING

	Matches	Innings	Not out	Runs	High score	Avg	100
Test	64	98	7	3,283	154	36.07	5
First class	979	1,532	85	58,969	305*	40.75	145

BOWLING AND FIELDING

	Runs	Wickets	Avg	5 W/I	10 W/M	BB	Ct	St
Test	2,815	83	33.91	4	1	7/76	64	0
First class	41,066	2,068	19.85	132	28	8/22	1,018	0

cricket heroes

INDEX

c r i c k e t   h e r o e s

INDEX

c r i c k e t   h e r o e s

INDEX

c r i c k e t   h e r o e s

INDEX

Picture credits

The publishers wish to thank the following sources for their help in providing the illustrations.

Allsport: 9, 94, 107, 110, 121, 139, 155, 187, 216
Adrian Murrell 31, 32, 42, 43, 89, 90, 91, 130, 212, 213
The Cricketer: 14, 15, 16, 19, 133, 147, 184, 200
Patrick Eagar: 22, 30, 33, 34, 35, 36, 37, 39, 40, 44, 48, 57, 61, 70, 88, 101, 129, 144, 145, 161, 166, 167, 168, 179, 190, 199, 214, 215
Mary Evans Picture Library: 92, 106, 115, 120, 140, 172
Hastings and St Leonard's Observer: 51
Keith Hayhurst Collection: 21
Hulton Deutsch: 10, 17, 20, 27, 29, 47, 50, 52, 53, 54, 55, 56, 59, 63, 64, 68, 72, 73, 74, 81, 82, 84, 85, 86, 93, 95, 102, 103, 118, 124, 126, 142, 143, 149, 157, 170, 171, 174, 177, 181, 188, 192, 194, 195, 202, 205, 209, 217, 218
Ken Kelly: 79, 98, 182, 183
Eamonn McCabe: 41
Press Association: 111, 112, 163, 165, 186
Sport & General: 75, 125, 137, 148, 158, 185
Surrey County Cricket Club: 146, 189
Sussex County Cricket Club: 162
Topham: 23, 25, 28, 60, 67, 77, 97, 100, 104, 123, 131, 150, 152, 156, 159, 175, 191, 197, 203
John Woodcock: 78
Tony Woodhouse (private collection): 108, 116

c r i c k e t   h e r o e s